HAUTE AND HOLY

THE HOUSE OF FAITH AND FASHION 2

TOBI RUBINSTEIN

Published by Citadelle Publishing LLC
Brooklyn, New York
www.citadellebooks.com

Cover Photo by Emily Jean Russell

Printed in the United States of America
ISBN 979-8-9859587-1-3
Citadelle Publishing LLc

Media inquiries info@thehouseoffaithandfashion.com

Photo courtesy of Iris Hyde

"Tobi has made faith her ultimate fashion statement that will never go out of style."

—Gedale Fenster

"What do faith and fashion have to do with each other? For many people, they see them on opposite ends of the spectrum of their daily lives. However, for Tobi Rubinstein, they are inherently linked in everything she does."

—Chicago Weekly News

"Tobi is about bringing greater awareness to faith and fashion." - **Fox**
"Imagine an electric mix of Carrie Bradshaw, Iris Apfel and the biblical Ruth would result in a most unusual triple threat trinity known as Tobi Rubinstein."

—Metropolitan Luxury Magazine

"An opus that takes a fresh new look at style and spirituality."

—DeMode Magazine

"Fashion, passion and Torah."

—Jewish Link

"As soon as I saw Tobi's interview, I knew I had to get her to do a fashion TV show for my network. I'm so excited to see how "The Fashion Four "will change the fashion media as she has chosen the most qualified and fabulous co-hosts."

—Natalie Cargile, Founder, The Connect Network TV

I dedicate this book to:

My husband, Felipe Orner, for being the
strength and love I have always needed.

"Te quiero con todo mi corazón."

My daughter, Lola Rubinstein, for giving me
complete joy in motherhood and in life.

And G-d for giving me the clear mission to keep going.

Haute and Holy: The House of Faith and Fashion 2, is a continuation of essays and conversations that fuse two subjects that should be opposed to each other yet live harmoniously within these pages. The goal of this book is to reveal G-d's presence in fashion, jewelry, beauty and lifestyle, viewed through the spiritual lens of Jewish and other religious teachings, therefore elevating the creative process by divine inspiration.

CONTENTS

"Paris is always a good idea."

Audrey Hepburn

Photo courtesy of Fashion Week Studio
Photographer: Alvin Toro

INTRODUCTION

As I stood in line backstage before one of the opening shows of Paris Fashion Week, I had to pinch myself to see if this wasn't an elaborate dream sequence. I leaned against the overly ornate stair rails leading to the red-carpet entrance of the venue in the Place Vendome Room in Paris's most prestigious and glamorous address, the iconic Ritz hotel. What was I doing there amidst all these very young, very tall, and very skinny models, practicing their prance before the producer gives them the cue to start walking the runway? I laughed at myself knowing that not only could I be their mother, but probably their grandmother as the age difference was so abundantly clear to everyone involved. As a newly acclaimed author, cancer survivor and G-d knows what else, never in my wildest dreams or bucket list musts did I think that I'd be walking the runway in Paris.

Last we left off from my first book, "The House of Faith and Fashion: What My Wardrobe Taught Me About G-d", I was in the midst of the battle of my life with stage 4 cancer. I am happy and grateful to report that after various kinds of medical treatments I am now cancer free, thank G-d.

However, what got me to Paris Fashion Week in March 2022 is a product of tenacity and trust in myself, and my newfound ability to appreciate every moment in my life as a gift-wrapped opportunity.

I confessed to my husband, Felipe, that I had a dream (where my ideas come from) that the cover of my next book was a photo of me walking down the runway in Paris. He jokingly said, "well Tobi, how are you going to accomplish that?" Since I love a good challenge, I put my plan into motion by calling the producer of Fashion Week Studio and invited him out to dinner. Over margherita pizzas in trendy Crowne Heights, Brooklyn (at the height of covid madness), I asked David Haines if there is any way that I can participate in their Paris Show. I shared my intent of using "the" photo for the cover of my next book. His expression was priceless as he conveyed how he loved the idea in so many different levels. He enthusiastically proclaimed, "It's about anti-ageism, it's about survival, it's about inclusiveness, it's about faith!" I didn't expect that kind of reaction that brought tears to my eyes. My giddiness took over completely. Did I just get myself into Paris Fashion Week as a model? Yep, you bet I did!

After I fully digested what I got myself into, I shared the idea with Mimixa Patel, my marketing consultant and we put the elaborate plan into motion. The popular Netflix series, 'Emily in Paris', became our inspiration as we branded the entire experience as 'Tobi in Paris' for the attendees and international press.

Friday, March 4, 2022, at 10am

"Dear Guest,

Thank you for attending the Opening Show for Fashion Week Studio at Salon Vendôme, The Ritz. Your presence today is even more meaningful for me, as I walk the runway in a Linda Sow dress with an Elizabeth Sutton clutch. As a recent stage 4 Uterine Cancer Survivor, Fashion Executive, Spiritual Warrior, Ceiling Crasher and a Best-Selling Author, it has been my dream to walk this runway, especially in Paris, sashaying in celebration of life, G-d and creativity.

You are all part of my book cover for The House of Faith and Fashion 2: 'Haute and Holy'.

Grateful beyond measure, À la santé et au bonheur,

Tobi Rubinstein"

I immediately sprang into action and hired Estie Duchman as my nutritional guide as I attempted to morph into a supermodel. She's the only one who can scold me into eliminating my favorite carbs and fats because we go back to first grade classmates at Bais Yaakov Queens. "Is that cookie really worth it??? Do you want to fit into that gown or not? After all you went through, you still want to have the same bad habits as before." Oiy, she can really bust up a good pizza binge, but she's the best in the game and a dear friend.

I almost felt sorry for Linda Sow, the designer, at our first fitting because she appeared so intensely nervous as she handed me her stunning black sequined gown with a hand stitched pearl neckline and ruffled hemline. Everyone in the surrounding area heard my huge scream of relief when I was comfortably zipped into her couture masterpiece!

After choosing a Tzuri Gueta necklace straight from his salon in Coulée Verte René-Dumont, and the 'STRONG' evening bag from Elizabeth Sutton, my runway look was complete.

The night before the big show, my husband carefully watched me practice walking in the hotel hallways with 3 different heights of black heels: 4 inches to massive platforms, from Manolos to Valentinos. Back and forth I went, trying not to slouch or fall. "You better work it girl" was playing on loop in my brain as I attempted to sashay in the corridor.

The entire Fashion Week Studio Inc staff, producers, dressers and makeup artists involved in the show were beyond accommodating to my religious practices which included arranging my appearance with ample time to prepare for Shabbos. I have endless gratitude and love for Tracey Murray, Amélie Pimont and Nathanaelle Hottois Galetlole (Founder & Owner of Fashion Week Studio) for making my dream come. G-d was orchestrating this event from above with the most glorious location paired with the most professional fashion teams.

Felipe Orner, my husband, adorned in a black French beret, escorted me down the red carpeted stairs to start my runway walk. The only thing I heard were roaring applause and flashing bulbs as I managed to make it straight and back in one piece. I took a bow and returned to Felipe in complete shock. Maybe I didn't drink enough water, or maybe I was just really hungry, but I was so lightheaded with joy and a real sense of accomplishment. I did it … I *really* did it.

That evening during the shabbat meal at the Chabad on the Champs Elysees, we realized that it had been one year since my big operation at Mount Sinai Hospital. They might have removed my ovaries and more, which left me with a huge ugly scar, but I just had the time of my life and the best picture for my next book (IYH) which you are reading right now.

FASHION WEEK

TOBI IN PARIS

Dear Guest,

Thank you for attending the Opening Show for Paris Fashion Week Studio at Salon Vandome, The Ritz. Your presence today is even more meaningful for me, as I walk the runway in a Linda Sow dress with an Elizabeth Sutton clutch. As a recent stage 4 Uterine Cancer Survivor, Fashion Executive, Spiritual Warrior, Ceiling Breaker and a Best Selling Author, it has been my dream to walk this runway, especially in Paris, sashaying in celebration of life, G-d and creativity.

You are all part of my book cover for
The House of Faith and Fashion 2:
'Haute and Holy'.

Grateful beyond measure,

À la santé et au bonheur.

Tobi Rubinstein

PARIS, FRANCE

FRIDAY, MARCH 4, 2022 | 10AM

SALON VANDOME | THE RITZ

In today's ever-evolving world, the realms of faith and fashion are no longer perceived as mutually exclusive. Instead, a growing trend of fusing these two seemingly distinct worlds has emerged, creating a harmonious blend that celebrates spirituality, individual expression, and cultural diversity. The combination of faith and fashion showcases how personal beliefs can be reflected in one's sense of style, leading to a profound impact on self-identity and a renewed appreciation for the divine in the world of aesthetics. G-d can be found in all creative spaces as this book continues to explore through the chapters of fashion, jewelry, style and beauty. The book is also filled with personal testimonies of G-d's presence in their crafts by the foremost leaders within these arenas.

The dance of faith and fashion is a transformative ballet. It transcends mere clothing choices and embraces the sacred essence of self-expression. From religious practices and modest fashion trends to eco-conscious and ethically sourced, the harmonious blend of faith and fashion reflects a profound shift in societal values. It celebrates individuality, while honoring the divine presence within us and the world that G-d created for us. As faith and fashion continue to intertwine, this powerful fusion serves as a reminder that true style lies not only in appearance but in the authenticity and reverence with which we express our inner beliefs, religious practices, spirituality, and deep gratitude to the original Creator.

I hope you enjoy Haute and Holy: The House of Faith and Fashion 2.

CHAPTER ONE

FASHION

"All who treat clothes with disrespect will end up not benefiting from them."

The Book of Traits by Rabbi Nachman

Photo courtesy of Mana Fashion Services

Mana From Heaven

The mere mention of the word "pagination" fused a friendship that might have started when she was an intern at Victoria's Secret, and I was a product manager for one of their suppliers. This was a history lesson in fashion catalogs that few people had or retained, but it was a language we both spoke.

Martu Freeman Parker was introduced to me by a mutual acquaintance in the modest fashion arena. Since I had moved partially to Miami, I thought it was best to meet the who's who of fashion. Well, Martu is the ruler of the who's who, and the mover and shaker of fashion in Miami as the matriarch of Mana Fashion Services. She is a great friend and kindred spirit as she shares ideals, work principals and creative outlets with me. We often brainstorm on groundbreaking ideas and events that truly broke the mold in fashion and continue to do so. What she and her fantastic team, Dominique Melul and Aleksandra Sivokoneva, are building for Mana Common is anything but common…it's extraordinary. Mana Common is a platform for urban revitalization and community building led and founded by its Chairman, Moishe Mana.

I had to include Martu in my book, as she is a living example of a master combination of faith and fashion.

Tobi, "Do you think that your creative talents are G-d given?"

Martu, "Absolutely! I believe I'm wired differently because of my creative talents. I believe everyone is put on this earth with an assignment and with talents and gifts to complete their assignment.

Tobi, "Any talent that sets you apart is not only G-d given, but also a superpower. You are building a fashion community in Miami, does that give you some G-d like qualities as He built the world? Why is it important for you to build it?"

Martu, "The vision to create a fashion community in Miami is G-d given. I believe so because my vision and the owner of Mana Common vision are perfectly aligned. Our goals and vision were identical. My journey to become the Managing Director for Mana Fashion Services was divine, all the pieces came together at once. Only G-d works so seamlessly. This project is not a small one or an easy one but the synergy of all involved is spiritual. Building a fashion community in south Florida allows creative people to connect, build and thrive together. I believe G-d wants that for all his children. I don't have G-d like qualities, but my vision and insight come from G-d. That is why I know building a fashion community in Miami is important."

Tobi, "How do you see faith and fashion as synergistic energies? Please give some examples."

Martu, "Faith and Fashion is a perfect marriage. In every religion, clothes are used to identify the important people. Religion uses fashion to tell stories, to keep history and traditions alive. Fashion is the most powerful form of expression. and Faith is how we express our love for G-d."

Tobi, "Do you need a lot of faith to be in the fashion industry? If so, what future do you see in its growth?"

Martu, "A strong faith system is absolutely necessary in the fashion industry. My faith always kept me grounded. This is an industry of excess, pride and vanity. You need a strong belief system to not let your talent be your G-d or worship other people's talents. I always knew to give all praises to G-d at all times. This would always humble me and put my assignment on this earth in perspective.

Tobi, "Mana Fashion was the host of the first Haute and Holy fashion show featuring modest fashion (during NYFW), why was that an important show to be a part of ?"

Martu, "The show gives G-d back the front row at NYFW. This show allowed designers to honor religion, tradition, and culture with fashion. Haute and Holy raised interest in people who did not understand modesty. But it also gave confirmation to the designer and the modest community that they are a part of the fashion industry. Haute and Holy showed how beautiful, chic, stylish, modern, classic and avant-garde modest fashion can be. I believe it canceled all the terrible stereotypes of modest fashion."

Tobi, "And it certainly did. How do you see the future of modesty fashion? What is your own personal practice of modesty?"

Martu, "I believe modesty fashion will become a choice for women all over the world. What I mean is more women will have more options to express themselves without feeling the need to reveal their entire body. The modest way of dressing can be sexy, stylish, classical, modern, chic and avant-garde. The more we see modest fashion shows, modest designers, and modesty in fashion publications the more normal modesty will become."

Tobi, "If you could design a prayer, what might that look like?"

Martu, "I honor you G-d with my talent, gifts and creativity every day of my life. I thank you for making me fully equipped to complete your assignment for me on earth. Amen"

"Mana from heaven" is an idiomatic expression that is often used to describe a situation where something unexpectedly good or beneficial happens at just the right moment. This phrase is often used in a figurative context to describe an unexpected windfall or a sudden solution to a problem that seemed insurmountable. The expression has roots in the Torah. Mana was the G-d given nourishment for the Israelites journey in the desert. It fell from heaven every day and twice on Friday for Shabbat. It was a miraculous meal that was a physical and spiritual cuisine that sustained them for 40 years.

Since then, the term "mana from heaven" has come to represent unexpected gifts or opportunities that seem to have come out of nowhere, leaving individuals feeling blessed and filled with gratitude.

Martu is mana from heaven.

Brand Identity

I watched Ralph Lauren's California Dreaming fashion show on Instagram live with all my senses engaged. His first west coast event was held at The Huntington Library, Art Museum, and Botanical Gardens in San Marino, California. The brand extravaganza encompassed all the reality and fantasy that has taken up real estate in my mind since I bought my first western themed ensemble in 1979. Editors, Hollywood elite and beloved family sat on benches and wicker chairs, observing the many facets of Lauren's empire—from Double RL to Purple Label. The styling of each mini collection showcased the wide breadth of what the world of Ralph has to offer. He has had a gigantic impact on every category of fashion. Après show dinner was served in the rose garden. The culinary scene was entirely bedecked with Ralph Lauren homewares; flatware and monogrammed charger plates to the tablecloths, cushions, and brass hurricanes that cast a poetic candlelit glow across the space, and not to mention the authentic Polo Bar menu. This evergreen brand has a complete universe of its own making. I am an active member of the RL society knowing well that it's the best marketing plan I've ever come across. Another confession: I have my original Ralph Lauren country chunky handknit wool pullover and wrap cardigan from the prairie collection circa 1983. This and so much more is a witness to how powerful the brand name is.

Founded by fashion designer and entrepreneur Ralph Lifshitz, this brand has become an enduring symbol of timeless elegance and American luxury. With its distinct fusion of classic design, impeccable craftsmanship, and aspirational lifestyle, the brand has left an indelible mark on the fashion industry. As a native New Yorker, he possessed a unique vision and an unwavering commitment to quality. His early career in the fashion industry allowed him to gain invaluable experience, which laid the foundation for his eponymous brand. Inspired by his love for classic aesthetics, Ralph Lauren sought to create a brand that epitomized sophistication and refinement while capturing the essence of the American spirit.

The brand became synonymous with its iconic logo, featuring a polo player on horseback. This distinctive emblem became a recognizable symbol of the brand's preppy, sporty, and aspirational image. It conveyed a sense of elegance, leisure, and adventure that resonated with consumers seeking to embody the quintessential American lifestyle.

I posed some questions exploring the power of a good name and a great brand to the Founder & Chairman of 5WPR, one of America's leading Public Relations agencies and top expert in his field, Ronn Torossian.

Tobi, "In Judaism, the power of a good name is the most important thing you can have, do you agree?"

Ronn, "A good name is very important. Names carry power and carry responsibility."

Tobi, "As the top PR person in the media today, can you define a "good name"?"

Ronn, "A good name is held by someone who is honorable, reliable and does the right thing. He or she needs to be an overall righteous person. However, this isn't entirely necessary, nor can it be easily measured in black and white. It has its interests in nuances and is filled with many layers."

Tobi, "Do you think that G-d needs a good PR firm now?"

Ronn, "I'm not sure G-d needs anything! Perhaps I propose the world and the media need more belief and fear of G-d. In my opinion, mankind's responsibility is acting good and carrying out good deeds."

Let's explore the significance of a good name in Judaism, as it's a part of a person's whole being.

"In life, you discover that people are called by three names: One is the name the person is called by his father and mother; one is the name people call him; and one is the name he acquires for himself. The best one is the one he acquires for himself." (Tanchuma, Vayak'heil 1)

The Hebrew translation of a good name is shem tov. As a shem tov, we should strive to set high standards for ourselves in how we act and behave towards others. In the book, 'Ethics of the Fathers', the scholar Hillel notes (chapter 2:7), "If you have acquired a good name, you had to do it yourself." In addition, Proverbs (22:1), "A good name is more desirable than great wealth, more even that silver or gold."

There is a Jewish tradition attributed to the kabalistic masters that one should recite a verse containing one's name or the first and last letters of one's name before stepping back at the conclusion of the silent Amidah (part of prayers three times a day). This is to remember one's name even in the hereafter. It is also a practice to add an extra letter to a sick person's name as an attempt to change their fate.

As per King Solomon, the wisest of all, "A good name is better than good oil" [Koheles 7:1]. The Medrash elaborates that the scent of good oil may linger for a while, however, a good name can carry a person across continents.

The concept of a good name is a universal idea that is present in many different religions and cultures. A good name is more than just a label for identification. It is believed to hold great significance and power, representing the character, identity, and potential of an individual.

This belief is observed in Christianity, where a name is viewed as an essential part of one's identity, reflecting their values and character. Throughout the scriptures, there are many stories of individuals who experienced a change of identity when their name was changed.

In Islam, a name is considered a gift from Allah and is chosen with the belief that it should have a positive meaning. It is also believed that a person's name can influence their destiny and a good name can bring blessings and protection.

Hinduism consults astrology for the baby naming process called Namkaran. According to Vedic astrology, your "rashi" is your moon sign, or the name of the zodiac position of the moon when you were born.

Even modern-day psychology practices hold that calling people by their name repeatedly affects their personality.

Overall, a good name is a powerful and an important component to yourself, inner, outer, and otherwise. Your name, which is your personal brand, reflect a world of possibilities.

"Each of us has a name given by G-d and given by our parents. Each of us has a name given by our stature and our smile and given by what we wear./ Each of us has a name given by the mountains and given by our walls./ Each of us has a name given by the stars and given by our neighbors./ Each of us has a name given by our sins and given by our longing./ Each of us has a name given by our enemies and given by our love./ Each of us has a name given by our celebrations and given by our work./ Each of us has a name given by the seasons and given by our blindness./ Each of us has a name given by the sea and given by our death." (Zelda, "Each Man Has a Name," as adapted by Marcia Falk in The Book of Blessings, New York: Harper Collins, 1996, p. 106ff.)

My name is Tobi, but my Hebrew name is "Tovah" and that means "good". What's yours?

Fashion Victim

The term "fashion victim" typically refers to someone who blindly follows every fashion trend without considering their personal style, comfort, or individuality. It describes a person who becomes excessively influenced by the latest fashion fads, often to the point of losing their own sense of style or identity. You have once been one or you definitely know one.

A fashion victim tends to prioritize being "on-trend" and conforming to popular fashion ideals rather than expressing their own unique personality and preferences. They may be overly concerned with labels, designer brands, and the opinions of others, valuing external validation over their own authentic self-expression. For example, being seen in Celine or perpetually in Prada!

However, it's essential to note that fashion is a form of self-expression and personal choice, and different individuals have varying approaches to it. While the term "fashion victim" carries a negative connotation, it's important to respect personal style choices and allow for individual preferences when it comes to fashion. But what happens when it's about hate? What if your favorite brand engages in hateful rhetoric fueled by a false pretense about your people, religion, or race? More specifically, Judaism.

The rise of antisemitism in recent years has been alarming, with the Jewish community being frequent target of hate crimes.

According to an FBI report, 63% of religious hate crimes target Jews, even though the Jewish community makes up for less than 2% of the U.S population. Antisemitism has been on a steady upward climb, with the last two years experiencing record spikes from physical harm to propaganda, and vitriol spewed on social media platforms. According to the NYPD, there has been a 21% increase in hate crimes in New York City this year compared to the same period last year, and most of those crimes were directed at Jews.

The white supremacist Proud Boys and Goyim Defense League, extreme sects of the Black Hebrew Israelite movement, and public figures including government representatives on both the far left and far right ends of the political spectrum, have also contributed to this surge in hate. Not to mention the Kanye affect and its lingering poison.

Sadly, Marc Jacobs, speaking out against antisemitism in an Instagram post (in October 2022) was one of the few major American designers to acknowledge the alarming rise in attacks against Jews across America.

The French luxury fashion house Louis Vuitton had been criticized by Israel advocates for hiring model Bella Hadid to be the face of its new collaboration with famed Japanese artist, Yayoi Kusama. The model's past antisemitic and anti-Israel remarks, and her participation in a pro-Palestinian rally that called for the destruction of Israel, which led to a massive hateful backlash towards Jews all over the world.

"It is imperative that influential people be held to account for their deeds and words," Malcolm Hoenlein, executive vice chairman of the Conference of Presidents of Major American Jewish Organizations, told The Algemeiner. "Ms. Hadid has repeatedly been identified with expressing hate promoting messages and inciting comments. LVMH should be particularly sensitive to this and should disassociate from her. Send a message that there will be no more no excuses, no exception. Jew hatred will not be tolerated."

In such circumstances, the fashion industry cannot be blind to bigotry. While it always stands up for communities facing bias and hate, the silence among big name talents has been deafening. Fashion designers should and must speak out against hate and call out antisemitism whenever and wherever they see it. That includes social media platforms and marketing campaigns that were generously afforded to other groups in similar situations. It is also important for the fashion industry to choose carefully whom they partner with and who will be the voice and face of their brands. They should cease relationships with those who are partaking in hate of any kind.

Ironically, the entire fashion industry, especially in New York (Garment District) has a rich and prosperous history with the Jews. The book, "A Perfect Fit: The Garment Industry and American Jewry, 1800-1960", explores the impact of the garment industry on American Jewry. It offers a comprehensive history of the American garment industry, covering its evolution from small-scale, handmade production to the large-scale factories that dominated the industry by the mid-20th century. Exploring how the industry provided economic and social opportunities for Jewish immigrants who were often excluded from other sectors of the economy due to anti-Semitism and discrimination. The organization of Jewish labor movement paved the roads to improving working conditions and wages for garment workers to form unions that exist till today.

The fashion world has a considerable platform to educate people about the real presence of antisemitism. The Council of Fashion Designers of America (CFDA) has come under scrutiny in recent years for its handling of alleged incidents of anti-Semitism. In 2019, designer Kerby Jean-Raymond accused the CFDA of systemic racism and anti-Semitism, citing incidents where he felt he was discriminated against because of his race and religion. Other Jewish designers have also spoken out about instances of anti-Semitism within the industry. In response to these concerns, the CFDA formed a new panel on inclusivity and diversity in 2019, which included several Jewish members. The panel was established to address issues of discrimination and bias within the industry and to promote greater diversity and inclusivity.

Despite the CFDA's efforts to address these issues, some members of the Jewish community remain skeptical. Some argue that the organization has not done enough to ensure that Jewish designers are not discriminated against or to hold members of the industry accountable for instances of anti-Semitism. Their efforts to address the issue through its diversity and inclusivity panel are a step in the right direction, but consistent and effective work remains to be done to ensure that Jewish designers and professionals can work in a safe environment.

So, before you shop for your "must have" designer brand of the moment, make damn sure that they align with your "must have" designer values as a Jew because no Jew deserves to be a victim of any kind.

G-d Walked the Runway

I had to catch it live on Instagram because I've been anticipating Pharrell's debut as Creative Director of Louis Vuitton since the formal announcement of his position. My obsession started way before I lectured about it with Fashion Group International (South Florida) in Miami. The success of his takeover of the acclaimed fashion brand was in my top three trend questions for 2023/24. "Pharrell was phor real" as I nearly dropped my phone in excitement many times during the live feed.

There was a massive gospel choir joined mid show after the orchestra played and the gritty rap music stopped. Their voices were a musical claim that after darkness, there comes light. The featured singer, clad in her Louis Vuitton white robe, sang "Thank G-d, and G-d is Joy". Did I just hear G-d at a major fashion show? Did I hear correctly? Praise G-d, I clearly did.

Gospel choirs play a significant role in contemporary Christian worship, particularly in African American churches in the United States. Gospel music is rooted in the traditions of African spiritual and gospel hymns, and it's characterized by its energetic rhythms, call-and-response patterns, and emphasis on vocal harmony. Many people see the act of singing gospel music as a way of communing with G-d and expressing one's faith and devotion. In this sense, gospel choirs play a key role in fostering a sense of community and togetherness. They provide a powerful and meaningful way for people to express their faith and devotion through music, and they contribute to the overall spiritual atmosphere of worship services and religious events.

This unprecedented entertainment was front and center at Louis Vuitton Men's Spring-Summer 2024 show on June 19 at Pont Neuf Bridge, Paris. "Pharrell's Louis Vuitton collection is enormous, for one, but also so quintessentially Pharrell that it feels less like Pharrell directing an LV collection and more like LV giving birth to Pharrell's wildest fashion dreams." writes Highsnobiety.

Louis Vuitton has a complicated history with Jewish people and Gypsies (also known as Roma). During the Nazi occupation of France, Vuitton was accused of collaborating with the enemy. In more recent years, Louis Vuitton has made efforts to acknowledge the darker chapters of its history. In 2019, the company invited Gypsy artist Ceija Stojka to create a series of artworks inspired by the brand's heritage. The company also established a partnership with the World Jewish Congress in 2011 to create a traveling exhibition that explored the role of Jewish people in the fashion industry.

Yet all seemed forgiven when Marc Jacobs, an American Jew served as the Creative Director for Louis Vuitton from 1997 to 2012. During his tenure at Louis Vuitton, Jacobs transformed the brand into a global powerhouse by infusing it with his own unique vision and style. One of Jacobs' signature achievements during his time at Louis Vuitton was the introduction of the brand's first-ever ready-to-wear clothing line. This was a departure from the brand's traditional focus on leather goods and accessories, and it helped to broaden the brand's appeal to a wider audience. Jacobs is also credited with rejuvenating Louis Vuitton's branding and marketing efforts. He collaborated with artists such as Stephen Sprouse and Takashi Murakami to create a limited-edition.

Virgil Abloh was Louis Vuitton's first African American Artistic Director, and one of the few black designers at the top of a French heritage house. Mr. Abloh, 37, was widely considered one of fashion's consummate purveyors of cool; a master of using irony, reference, and the self-aware wink. He was the master collaborators mixing LV with the biggest brands from street wear to master artists. His sudden death left a huge hole for LVMH, as his sneakers would not be easily filled.

The world was a little skeptical with the company's next choice of Pharrell, for he is known only as a popular singer and multiple brand ambassador. "I'm the second Black man to ever experience this on the planet, the biggest fashion house in the world," Williams said in an interview with Reuters before the show, referring to his job since February.

Models strode across a runway to live music, parading pearl-embellished tracksuits, furry outerwear, and sparkling jackets with checkmarks in all colors and sizes. An audience gathered along the Seine River craned to catch a glimpse of the show which continued LV's approach of mixing street style with luxury.

I'm not sure if there were more A-list celebrities watching or well-tailored models walking the golden bridge of eternal branding. The show ended with a great act of humility, gratitude, and a bow as Pharrell honored all the teams that worked to make this magnificent collection and show happen. This was a finale that only G-d could have orchestrated. G-d was the most important guest in the house of Louis Vuitton that day, and to that I say, "Praise the Lord".

LBD

Black is not my favorite color, but I do have a favorite LBD, or little black dress. Yet mine is a little more than that... It's a black lace vintage Emanuel Ungaro from his shop in Paris circa the 1980s. The craftsmanship is so luxurious that I can just display it on my door and stare at it as a work of art. The details of ruffle layers backed with nude silk and intricate jet beading are luscious. I love that dress, as it's a gift from Donna Schneier's personal wardrobe that I truly cherish.

What's up with the importance of our little black dress? Is it because black hides everything? Or is black slimming? Or are we too lazy to find anything else?

The term "little black dress" (often abbreviated as LBD) refers to a versatile and timeless style of women's dress that is typically simple, elegant, and black in color. The concept of the little black dress originated in the fashion industry and has become a staple in many women's wardrobes. This dress is characterized by its versatility and ability to be dressed up or down for various occasions. It is often seen as a reliable go-to option for events ranging from casual gatherings to formal occasions. The simplicity and neutral color of the dress allow for flexibility in accessorizing and pairing it with different shoes, jewelry, and outerwear.

Like they say, "when in doubt, wear black".

The LBD gained popularity in the early 20th century, thanks in part to the influence of fashion icon Coco Chanel. Chanel popularized the concept of the dress as a wardrobe staple, describing it as a versatile and essential piece that every woman should have in her closet.

However, black is certainly a popular color choice in Jewish communities. I really can't find any laws that require the color to dominate your wardrobe, so I'm just going to say "maybe" these are the reasons.

Maybe wearing black clothing is seen as a way to promote modesty in appearance. Black garments are considered unassuming and less likely to attract attention or focus on one's physical appearance. Certainly, the choice of black clothing among Orthodox and Hasidic Jewish women is deeply rooted in longstanding customs and traditions. These communities follow specific guidelines regarding modest dress, and black attire aligns with these.

In some Christian traditions, priests, nuns, and monks wear black clothing as a sign of their religious vocation and commitment to serve the church and communities.

Within Islam, the burqa is a type of outer garment worn by some Muslim women as part of their religious and cultural practices. It is typically a loose-fitting, full-body covering that includes a mesh screen or grille over the face, often leaving only the eyes visible. The color of the burqa can vary depending on cultural traditions and personal preferences. While black is a commonly seen color for burqas, it is not exclusive to the garment. Burqas can be found in different colors.

The color black has so much more to offer than just a uniform of any kind, whether religious, cultural, or a choice of dress.

Rabbi Yehuda Surpin wrote an article on Chabad.org explaining black beautifully: "According to physics, black is not actually a color; it is the absence of light that appears black. From the standpoint of dyes and pigments, black absorbs all light and doesn't reflect any colors back (in other words, again, you aren't seeing any color)." He writes further, "This unique property of the color black symbolizes Gd's absolute unity, oneness that does not lend itself to any additional attributes or parts."

In light of this, black just might be my new favorite color—or not a color at all.

Killer Clothes

My stepson, Eli Orner, bought me a book that he knew would touch me deeply.

"The Seamstress of Auschwitz" is a historical fiction novel that takes place in the context of one of the darkest times of human history, the Holocaust. The story centers around a young woman named Ada, who is taken to Auschwitz along with her mother and younger brother. Ada is forced to work at the camp's fashion department (hard to believe there is one) due to her sewing skills and eventually becomes the personal seamstress of the camp commander's wife.

The novel provides a vivid portrayal of life inside the concentration camp and the extreme horrors that the prisoners faced. Due to the shortage of materials, Ada is tasked with creating beautiful clothes from scraps of fabric and other materials. The author portrays Ada's resistance against the camp authorities by sewing secret messages and symbols into the clothing that she makes. Through Ada's character, the author highlights the resilience and determination of people under extreme circumstances. The story is heart-wrenching, with moments of hope and humanity interspersed throughout. In particular, Ada's character is deeply compelling as she struggles to maintain her integrity and resist the acts of violence and hatred happening around her.

As a Jewish woman, it's difficult to digest that there was a haute couture sewing workshop in the heart of Auschwitz. Could there be anything more disturbing than knowing that starving, broken, and enslaved Jewish women were working to keep Nazi wives well dressed? Can there be any other description for an ensemble produced there other than "killer clothes"?

The perpetrators of the Final Solution exhibited a greater interest in Jewish plunder than in Jewish lives, and high-ranking Nazi officials and their families didn't mind donning clothing fashioned by those they regarded as no better than pests. The Upper Tailoring Studio, established within the confines of Auschwitz, illustrates this despicable extravagance. Numerous individuals were coerced into operating sewing workshops in ghettos and concentration camps during the Second World War. Yet, this particular workshop was not established to produce or repair military garments. It was instead formed exclusively for a prissy elite who indulged their love for fashion in the midst of an infernal existence.

Hedwig Hoess, the wife of the Auschwitz commandant, recruited her first two local Polish seamstresses to work at her villa, which overlooked the concentration camp. This was situated next to the mammoth warehouses of confiscated goods. As prisoners labored to process these goods, they often stumbled across possessions belonging to their own dead family. Hedwig initially drew disdain from other female officers and the wives of officers due to her lavish clothing collection. She responded to their jealousy by establishing the elite Upper Tailoring Studio within the camp's limits.

There were also esteemed labels that took advantage of the Holocaust. Hugo Ferdinand Boss, the founder of Hugo Boss, was known to have produced SS uniforms as early as 1934 and was a member of the Nazi party. Similarly, Pierre Cardin, a famous French designer, used forced labor from Jewish prisoners at the Salon du Prêt-à-Porter during the German occupation of France. Other fashion labels, including Rochas, Hermès, and Lanvin, used forced labor during the war, although the extent and details of their actions are less well documented or better hidden.

This is a very dark chapter in the history of the fashion industry. Many of these companies have since apologized for their actions, but the legacy of this exploitation lingers and begs the question, "At what price do you pay for killer clothes?"

Woman of Valor

I was startled when the presenter from Pantone Color Experts quoted an excerpt from Proverbs. I inquired about her point of view concerning an upcoming museum project surrounding faith and fashion at St. Thomas University (scheduled for Fall 2024). I did not expect her to answer me with lines from the poem "Women of Valor". "She makes herself clothes of linen and purple and coats her home with scarlet." That's an impressive comeback for my inquiry. Especially since she just finished a presentation forecasting the season's "must-have" colors to a room full of fashion enthusiasts at the Mana Fashion Services Miami headquarters.

Here is the poem in its entirety:

Proverbs 31:10--31

A woman of valor, who can find? For her price is far above rubies. The heart of her husband safely trusts in her, and he has no lack of gain. She does him good and not evil all the days of her life. She seeks wool and flax and works willingly with her hands. She is like the merchant ships; she brings her food from afar. She rises also while it is yet night, and gives food to her household, and a portion to her maidens. She considers a field and buys it; with the fruit of her hands, she plants a vineyard. She girds her loins with strength and makes strong her arms. She perceives that her merchandise is good; her lamp goes not out by night. She lays her hands to the distaff, and her hands hold the spindle. She stretches out her hand to the poor; Yea, she reaches forth her hands to the needy. She is not afraid of the snow for her household; For all her household are clothed with scarlet. She makes for herself coverlets; Her clothing is fine linen and purple. Her husband is known in the gates, when he sits among the elders of the land. She makes linen garments and sells them; and delivers girdles unto the merchant. Strength and dignity are her clothing; and she laughs at the time to come. She opens her mouth with wisdom; And the law of kindness is on her tongue. She looks well to the ways of her household and eats not the bread of idleness. Her children rise up, and call her blessed; Her husband also, and he praises her:' Many daughters have done valiantly, But you rise above them all.' Grace is deceitful, and beauty is vain; But a woman that fears the LORD, she shall be praised. Give her of the fruit of her hands; And let her works praise her in the gates.

Eshet Chayil (pronounced AISH-ET CHAI-EEL or EISHES CHAYIL) is generally translated as "Woman of Valor." It's a portion from the Book of Proverbs (chapter 31:10–31) that is traditionally sung before the Friday night Shabbat meal from husband to wife, just before Kiddush, as an honorable hymn to the mother or matriarch of the family.

If you read it carefully, it sums up a woman who can do everything—the original superwoman. She runs her household, works in the garment trade, and is a partner with her husband. She's a quiet force of fierceness clothed in purple linen. She is a selfless, humble, and powerful mother and wife. She is, after all, priceless!

Do you know any women like that? I sure don't. None of my friends or colleagues could ever measure up to the woman described in this song. In addition, I don't know any husbands who really think their wives are renditions of this poem. My friend Sharon, a Jewish orthodox feminist, summed up her personal description of what an Eshet Chayil is by celebrating her multifaceted identities and by unapologetically breaking barriers.

Yet, I must confess that over the years I have longed for a husband to sing this to me and actually mean every word, and Thank G-d I finally did. Ok, he might be fibbing a bit (a lot), but some parts are true, and some parts will never be true. Yet it's the ideal and the idea that really count. I'm known to joke that perhaps the Rabbis should switch out this song for "Song of Songs" by King David because it's the romantic version of a relationship instead of the practical mechanics offered here.

What is this superwoman anyway?

The Eshet Chayil is a powerhouse. She has been at the forefront of Jewish spiritual and communal growth since her inception. King Solomon, the author of this poem, shatters the image of a hidden identity for women and puts her at the forefront of the family.

Before the Torah was given on Mount Sinai, Moses presented it to the women first, signifying their primary role in birthing and educating the nation.

According to the Talmud, women were created with an extra dose of wisdom and understanding, called binah yeteirah. This is deeper than "women's intuition"; it is the ability to have a thorough understanding from every angle.

I think there might be a new version of a woman of valor who is setting her own standards of superwomanhood. In late 2020, Gal Gadot (Marvel's Superwoman) was named the new global ambassador for luxury jewelry brand Tiffany & Co. Gadot was selected as a representative of the brand's belief in empowerment and optimism, which she embodies through her on-screen roles and off-screen philanthropy work. She has become a fashion role model due to her unique sense of style, empowerment, versatility, individuality, and commitment to promoting sustainable fashion. She is a symbol of confidence, creativity, and strength on and off the screen, whether as a comic book character or in real life. She's also proud of her Judaism, proud of her country, Israel, the first of her kind to receive a star on the Hollywood Walk of Fame, and soon to be Cleopatra.

Ok, we all can't be Gal Gadot, but we can be our best selves, defying conventional expectations, redefining roles, and embracing our true G-d given gifts.

Blue Genes

The most staple piece in any fashion wardrobe has got to be a pair of jeans. For me, my jeans have outfitted me through a religious journey of obedience, rebellion, and complete surrender. My hip-hugging bell bottoms were hidden under my long skirts in high school. My designer jeans walked me through marriages and divorces. My skinny jeans were sacrificed as a deal I made with G-d over cancer recovery. Now I am left with a box full of them to be worn as leggings because I can't give them up entirely.

Our love affair with blue jeans is a serious and lifelong relationship, but Jews and jeans go way back.

In 1829, Levi Strauss, the founder of the iconic denim brand Levi's, was born into a Jewish family in Germany. He later emigrated to the United States, settling in San Francisco, California, and starting his work-related utility pant company, also known as denim blue jeans. The brand has defined the standard of fit and quality to this very day as it continues to evolve and stay current.

The famous Sassoon family also designed a line of jeans, along with the Nakash brothers and their Jordache Enterprises. Those two brands dominated the 1970s and 1980s.

Yet my favorite and my one-time FIT professor, Calvin Klein, took his signature jean company to another level. If I ever meet him again, I will tell him that I used to see him eat lunch with his dad at the kosher dairy restaurant on the corner of 28th Street and 7th Avenue. Klein pushed the boundaries of what was acceptable in the fashion industry, and his designs were often provocative and controversial, starting with the Brooke Shields ad campaign.

What's so intriguing about the color blue?

The indigo dye, synonymous with denim, is deeply ingrained in our collective fashion consciousness, symbolizing rebellion, authenticity, and freedom.

In the realm of fashion, color holds a significant place, capable of evoking emotions, making statements, and defining trends. Among the diverse palettes available, blue stands out as an enduring favorite, particularly associated with denim blue.

Blue exudes a sense of calmness, tranquility, and reliability. It represents serenity, stability, and trust, making it an ideal choice for fashion. Whether it's a vibrant shade of cobalt or a soothing hue of baby blue, this color can effortlessly capture attention, making a bold yet composed statement. In fashion, blue is often associated with elegance, sophistication, and a timeless appeal, thus enhancing the overall aesthetic of clothing.

This all has its origins in the Torah. What is the biblical term Tekhelet and the holy color blue?

G-d designed the prayer shawl with two kinds of thread attached to the corners, in white and blue cloth (perhaps wool). The colored singular fringe was known as Tekhelet. It was the visual hallmark of nobility and in line with the purpose of reminding the Jewish male that he is a member of G-d's kingdom of priests. G-d commands the following instructions: "Speak to the children of Israel, and you shall say to them that they shall make for themselves fringes (tzitzit) on the corners of their garments, throughout their generations, and that they shall affix a thread of Tekhelet on the fringe of each corner."

The unique blue dye was made from a byproduct of a sea creature known as the chilazon, which lived in the Mediterranean Sea. It surfaced every seven years and became extinct approximately a thousand years ago. Recently, the marine snail Murex trunculus has been identified as possibly being the elusive chilazon, and many use its dye today. However, it's been said that the authentic version of the Techlis will not return until the Messiah arrives.

How remarkable is the biblical color of blue? Rabbi Meir would ask, "What makes T'chelet different from other colors? – T'chelet is similar in color to the sea, and the sea is comparable to the sky, and the sky to the throne of (G-d's) presence" (Menachot 43b).

As far as I'm concerned, that's a blue worth waiting for, but until then, I'll wear my jeans underneath my dress and continue to pray for the Messiah to arrive!

Reflecting Modesty

According to marketing firm MLC Media, the modest fashion apparel segment is poised to reach $360 billion globally over the next two years. Every emerging trend report I've read has taken a stand for the growth of modest mode. At a Fashion Group International gathering in Miami, I stated in a 2023–24 market report that I saw more covered-up models on the runways than stripped-down ones. I laugh at the comeback of the long denim skirt labeled "Torah Teacher Chic" by Vogue. There isn't a yeshivah girl in the world who hasn't worn one of those skirts in her lifetime. As for the shows I saw in Paris Couture Week this past July, the trend is growing exponentially, as reflected by Tom Brown, Chanel, Fendi, and more.

While being interviewed for Forbes, the writer Stephan Rabimov asked me to share my thoughts on up-and-coming "modest changemakers". I stated in the article, "Whether it be in Judaism, Islam, or even some Christian sects, contemporary religious connotations can easily be adhered to with so many fashion choices driven by the emerging force of modest influencers such as The Reflective."

The Reflective are sidelining religion and making modesty mainstream, therefore reaching a wider audience with their message. They crush stereotypes, a superpower I admire the most. Liza Sakhaie and Danielle Immerman named their shopping platform The Reflective because "We believe modesty can and should reflect your personality. Modesty can and should reflect your authentic self. Modesty can and should reflect your confidence."

They were among the first people that I contacted to share my thoughts on writing Book 2 and continuing the dialogue about faith and fashion. Here are some of their thoughts that speak to me the most:

LIZA SAKHAIE

"I spent 10 years in the fashion industry surrounded by shallow vanity, inspiring me to seek a way to give clothing meaning without my body as the focus. However, I noticed my personality disappear with a more conservative style, so I embarked on a journey of discovering modest ways to wear the styles I always felt most confident in: jeans, pant suits, and camisole dresses. It's OUR MISSION to share products and style secrets with every MODEST woman."

ARIELLA IMMERMAN

"I never considered myself fashionable until I started dressing modestly four years ago. With fewer products and styles at my disposal, I began searching for pieces that felt like a true representation of my personality and that I felt good in. In that search, I found freedom in expression and freedom to be me. Our mission is to inspire this enjoyment, satisfaction, and confidence for all modest women."

With a company mission such as theirs, I knew the dialogue had to be continued with these questions.

Tobi, "Did you need faith in order to launch The Reflective? Did G-d play a role in it?"

Liza and Ariella, "Faith definitely played a role in launching The Reflective, from our personal faith in the concept of modesty to our faith in the idea that a better modest shopping experience could exist. Throughout the past three years of building The Reflective, there were undoubtedly times when we struggled and times when it felt like we were doing an impossible task. What kept us going was reminding ourselves that we aren't building this website and community for ourselves or from a place of ego; we genuinely set out to create a solution for modest women everywhere and to help modest women everywhere. With that in mind, we always released the outcome of our success with full trust and faith that G-d would and would help us succeed for the pure purpose of creating a beautiful and easy modest fashion experience for women of all faiths and backgrounds."

Tobi, "Choosing the modest category of fashion is quite limiting; why did you select such a narrow space? Or has that space truly widened?"

Liza and Ariella, "Over the last five years, the modest fashion space has evolved and widened a great deal and will only continue to expand in the years to come as the modest dressing population grows and the fashion industry evolves. Every year, modesty continues to be a trend in the mainstream fashion industry; from midi skirts taking off four years ago to maxi hemlines sweeping the runways in the last year, we continuously see Vogue and industry publications cite modest styles as major trends. We've been waiting for these modest moments to diminish in mainstream fashion, but they only continue to persevere and rise, with this season seeing a particularly strong uptick with quiet luxury, which tends to be more modest, a more covered look as a whole being a trend in itself, and maxi hemlines reigning as the skirt of choice. We anticipate modesty to continue growing as a space within mainstream fashion."

Tobi, "What do you want to achieve in the next 5 years with your newly revised website? That is what I call a Net-A-Porter for modest attire..."

Liza and Ariella, "We hope to continue growing our community and reach to provide more women with the opportunity to enjoy an easy modest shopping experience while simultaneously working to improve that modest shopping experience through a variety of brands, including more plus-size, maternity, and sustainable options for our community. Similarly, in the same way sustainability and plus-size fashion have become top-of-mind needs for mainstream fashion to address, we hope that modest fashion can find a space in industry demand."

Clearly, these two understood the assignment and made modesty a mode more marvelous than ever before.

In the Nude

I looked at the lady who was stacking the yogurts next to the assorted kosher cheeses as she surveyed the black fishnet stocking that blazed by en route to the back of the mart. Just before I could share her smirk, another version in white followed suit, with the last one sashaying her way back to the bakery section. Before I start laughing again, let me go into some details. I am referring to three females, identified as females, or I'm trying really hard to be a female, who walked into a kosher supermarket on a Friday at noontime. They were displaying almost-nude outfits to order a pizza and obviously gather as much attention as possible. You couldn't miss their smiley-face nipple covers over their thongs. Every customer, clerk, stock person, butcher, baker, and sushi maker had a bird's-eye view. I couldn't stop laughing as I watched all this play out, including the shocked expression of the cashier. What started out as a mission by this trio ended as a comedy sketch. They wanted desperately to cause a scene of envy, lust, and seduction and finished with a kosher extra-cheese pizza and severely deflated egos.

I knew this had to be part of my essay about the power of nude looks on the runways, red carpets, and beyond. Let's undress this.

Nude dressing, or wearing garments that create the illusion of nudity, can be seen as empowering for several reasons. Choosing to wear a nude dress can be a way for individuals to express their personal style and confidence. It allows people to showcase their comfort with their bodies and celebrate their unique beauty. Embracing nude dressing can promote body positivity by challenging societal norms and taboos.

It can be a rebellious symbol against conventional beauty standards.

It's a favorite among the Hollywood types attending red carpet parties and industry events. Julia Fox extended her career (after being Kanye's girlfriend for 15 minutes) by making sure her naked outfits got more outrageous with every paparazzi post. Leaving her fans with the question, "What's left to show?"

The concept of covering the nude body in Judaism is subject to the laws of modesty; the same is true for the Muslim faith. Covering body parts is not only about temptation. It is about how women view themselves and the respect they have for their own bodies, which are considered sacred and precious creations of G-d. In fact, modesty is applied to men's bodies as well, although it is even more important for women's bodies, which are seen as having a deeper beauty and a greater spiritual source. This belief is supported by the Kabbalists, who teach that a woman's soul comes from a higher place and is thus reflected in her physicality. Modesty is not a sign of shame or inferiority; it is an expression of reverence and admiration.

The Torah, the sacred Jewish text, is treated in a similar manner. It is housed in a beautiful ark, wrapped in multiple layers, and only brought out three times a week during prayers. This is not because it is shameful or ugly, but because it is too precious to be treated casually. By keeping it out of sight, its sanctity is preserved and respected. The same is true for the human body, which is also considered to be a holy creation of G-d. By keeping it covered, we maintain our reverence and respect for ourselves and for each other. In a world where the exposure of the female body has become a cheap marketing tool, the sacredness of the body has been lost. But within the Jewish tradition, we are reminded that which is truly precious to us, we keep under wraps.

During NYFW, the idea of introducing a purely modest event was something never done before and surely against the nudity trend on other runways. Teaming up with Mana Fashion Services and the most creative designers, producers, beauty teams, and media partners, we took the task to the fashion public. The afternoon was filled with informative talks, pop-ups, and a runway show that incorporated Muslim, Christian, and Jewish designers with the common theme of "covering up".

AM New York wrote:

"While nudity was a trend on the runways during New York Fashion Week with Prabal Gurung, the opposite held true at "Haute and Holy," presented by Mana Fashion Services.

The modest fashion event brought together 120 fashionistas and influencers from varying religious denominations. The organizers presented a runway of colorful splendor that celebrated the intersection of styles and faiths."

Modesty had made it to NYFW, and the response was glorious.

There is an alternative to nude, an anti-nude movement called modest. It appears to be quite the opposite end of the spectrum, but the fashion pendulum is beginning to swing in the other direction.

No, you don't have to show all to be ALL. You don't have to reveal yourself to steal the spotlight. You don't have to strip to make hearts skip. You don't have to be nearly nude to exude who you really are.

Swim Weak

Panama may have the best kosher restaurants in the world, but they also have the best modest swimwear.

A Panamanian brand, Formentera Swimwear, was created to fill the need for chic, covered, and easy swimwear with ensembles that belong on the beaches of St. Tropez. The exclusive print bathing suits and matching sarongs are the most glamorous getups to make an impression at any pool, anywhere in the world. The brand is more than a water wardrobe; it's a fashion lover's dream of covering up without looking like a scuba diver. Covering up has gone completely chic, and leave it up to the Latin women to figure that one out!

It's certainly a tricky place to lounge poolside if you adhere to modesty laws within the Jewish and Muslim communities. How do you handle the tiki bar while sitting next to a string bikini? What do you do under the cabana at the Copacabana with your pina colada? Do you just throw a blanket over your head and pray that nobody notices? Fret not, for Formentera has something amazing for the Amalfi Coast.

Covering up at any beach, resort, or pool isn't an easy task considering all the rules, and there could be lots of them depending on how strict the community is.

Surprisingly, the hashtag '#modestswimwear' received 16 million views in 2022, as opposed to 2 million in the past years.

In various Orthodox Jewish communities, there may be separate swimming arrangements for men and women to maintain modesty and uphold religious customs. This practice aims to provide separate spaces for men and women to swim comfortably. There are destinations with "women or men only" beaches. All these accommodations are almost identical in the Muslim communities as well. In some parts of the Middle East, there are "women only" beach clubs.

Why did these amazing designers, Rachel Schwartz and Perla Nessim, choose such a difficult task as modest swimwear? I asked Rachel...

Tobi, "What propelled you to enter the modest swimwear market?"

Rachel, "Definitely the necessity for it! The void in the market for modest swimwear three years ago was really big. Living in the tropics, going to the pool or beach very often was truly a struggle for me, so I decided to create what I would have loved to see in a store!"

Tobi, "Do you believe your talents are G-d given?"

Rachel, "Yes 100% I believe G-d gives special talents to each person, and it's up to us to develop and exploit them."

Tobi, "Modesty practices are especially difficult in swimwear; how do you make it fun and exciting enough to complete with traditional swimsuits?"

Rachel, "We always try to be on trend so modest girls don't feel they are being "left out"! We truly invest a lot of time and effort designing the prints, so they are fancy and attractive to make our customer feel beyond gorgeous!"

Tobi, "What are your thoughts about modest swimwear being shown in Miss Universe pageant contestants as Miss Bahrain?"

Rachel, "I believe modesty is getting more popular by the minute. Modesty is elegance, and modesty is royalty. It doesn't really surprise me as she represents her country and her culture."

Tobi, "If the biblical Batya wore swimwear to bathe in the Nile, how would you design her ensemble?"

Rachel, "I would make her a midi kaftan with flowy sleeves in a beautiful botanical print."

I imagine that Pharaoh's daughter, Princess Batya, would look stunning as she scooped up the basket that held Baby Moses!

My personal relationships with bathing suits are sometimes very complicated. When I try one on, I don't even want to exit the fitting room, let alone attempt a swim in my own pool. Swimwear has an anxiety level all its own, and depending on my weight, workout, and self-esteem issues, I tend to avoid this fashion category all together these days. I would rather close my eyes and imagine my teenage self as a swimsuit-fit model for AH Schreiber and Company. That brings me all the joy I need right now.

There was a Nun and a Rabbi

Sometimes reality is a lot more unbelievable than fiction. Why bother developing fake news when real-life happenings can be a lot more interesting? In November 2022, I was invited to an inaugural Faith and Fashion program hosted by St. Thomas University Fashion School in Miami. It became a movie script that even I couldn't have written any better.

It was humorous enough for a Jewish Orthodox female, a Rabbi, and an ex-Rebbetzin to be lecturing at a Catholic university's fashion school. The experience was only matched by being blessed by a nun, greeted by a Father, and having the Chabad campus Rabbi and Rebbetzin in the audience. The concept of the unusual program was the brainchild of Ashlee Rzyczycki, Program Director and Assistant Professor of the Fashion Merchandising Program at St. Thomas University.

We became kindred soul sisters during our first conversation as panelists for a modest fashion event at Mana Fashion Services in downtown Miami. She then followed up with her own faith and fashion forum at the university. The questions she scripted for our "talk show" discussion that day were so thoughtful. It shocked me, as I didn't expect the sensitivity and candidness of the subject matter. Most particularly about one wedding dress that was used in a Displaced Persons Camp after the Holocaust. Everything about that program gave me insight into her depth, which led me to ask deeper questions.

Tobi, "Why are you so interested in fusing faith and fashion? Please give some examples."

Ashlee, "Growing up in a strict Catholic household, I have always been very spiritual. My parents always instilled in me the importance of dressing conservatively and valuing modesty. I also went to Catholic schools that required uniforms. Wearing a uniform taught me valuable lessons about not building an identity through clothing for others to view me in a certain way but using it as a way of self-expression. Through my faith-based education, I learned that, and I genuinely believe that to be a gift from G-d.

I also had religion intertwined with fashion growing up, but it could have been more apparent. Ideals of trying not to have excess because of what the Bible tells us, not to be wasteful, or give our outgrown clothing to those in need within our communities. These were always lessons I was taught about the impact of clothing. I always lived with a sense of morality and tried to be a good person; fashion also played a role in that.

College was also a very important part of my fashion journey. I majored in art therapy and wanted to help people. I did an internship and realized art therapy wasn't for me. I was still determining what path to pursue. I had grown up in a house that reused and recycled (before anybody else did it), and I also took sewing lessons as a child. I didn't even think I could major in fashion or do something I loved. I switched majors my junior year. I knew that whatever I did in fashion, I wanted to help people or do something good. I believe that to be G-d's plan for me. After learning about fashion, understanding it, and integrating my faith, I also found a way to express myself through clothing.

Colossians 3:12: "Therefore, as G-d's chosen ones, holy and beloved, clothe yourselves with compassion, kindness, humility, meekness, and patience." Fashion helps me to remember that it is more than the external message of what people think on the outside; it is also important to remember what is important on the inside."

Tobi, "Do you think it's a G-d given mission that you are manifesting?"

Ashlee, "I never knew that this would be my mission. There has been a movement toward modesty; for some time, many people just associated it with specific religions. However, it always resonated with me, coming from a Catholic background. Being modest doesn't mean you can't dress beautifully. I remember hearing you for the first time. Everything about your book—the lessons associated with G-d and the connection to fashion—resonated with me. Something clicked in me so that I could teach my students along the same lines. I had been teaching my students how to be good people and to make a difference in the fashion industry. Listening to how you incorporate beautiful lessons from G-d into Fashion teaches us the lessons G-d wants us to know and aligns them with fashion. It was like a bolt of lightning. It makes my mission so much more defined to be able to align these elements into what I teach, despite being an unpopular concept. It is what I believe, and I am incredibly passionate about it, as you are, Tobi. It makes me realize that this is the path G-d wanted me to go on, and that I can make a difference in my students lives. As you say, "G-d is the original couturier," why not teach my students how Faith and Fashion connect? I hope that message will resonate with my students to truly have G-d in their hearts to help them make sound ethical decisions when they are in the industry."

Tobi, "How does it feel to be teaching Fashion in a faith-based school?"

Ashlee, "Teaching at faith-based schools is so important to me. Having a discussion involving G-d at an accepted place is my passion and a big part of my identity. Also, having conversations about G-d and faith is acceptable at a faith-based school, which isn't the case at many Universities. Having religion and spirituality is a part of who I am, and being at a school where it is safe to teach these valuable lessons is extremely rewarding and my mission in life. I can't imagine teaching anywhere else. Teaching students to have faith and spirituality is important to ensure that the next generation of leaders are making decisions to better the lives of others around them; being servant leaders."

Tobi, "Please share a preview of the upcoming museum installation of Faith and Fashion that we are doing together."

Ashlee, "It is essential to bridge gaps between all faiths. So many disputes happen because people do not understand each other. I have learned so much about Judaism through my conversations with you. I have also been inspired by what you mentioned as your first inspiration behind Faith and Fashion. Heavenly Bodies was an exhibit at the Metropolitan Museum of Art that encompassed holy vestments and fashions inspired by the Catholic Church. You and I began discussing the possibility of merging Judaism and Catholicism to provide an exhibition to teach the history behind the holy vestments and lessons learned in both faiths about fashion. We are trying to continue the conversation we have had about integrating faith and fashion and reaching a wider audience. We have approached religious leaders in both the Jewish and Catholic communities, and they are excited and motivated to do an exhibit in September 2024. I am so glad to be working on this with you because you inspire me, and I cannot ask for a better ally to continue this mission. I think G-d brought us together for a reason."

In both Christianity and Judaism, the commonality of emphasizing modesty in faith and fashion is pivotal in creating and upholding a respectful environment within their respective religious communities. This shared emphasis underscores the importance of dressing modestly when attending religious services, reflecting a reverence for sacred spaces and practices. The modest dress code promotes a focus on inner virtues and humility, allowing individuals to connect deeply with their spirituality. Moreover, by adhering to these principles, members of these communities foster a sense of inclusivity and unity, as everyone shares similar standards in their attire. Additionally, embracing modesty in both faith and fashion serves as a visible marker of cultural and religious identity, preserving and celebrating age-old traditions.

Promoting unity through education is a powerful means of bringing diverse individuals together and fostering understanding, empathy, and a shared sense of purpose. By providing access to quality education, societies can break down barriers, bridge cultural divides, and encourage collaboration towards common goals. Education nurtures tolerance and respect for different perspectives, cultivating a harmonious environment where people can coexist, learn from one another, and work collectively to address global challenges. Through shared knowledge and experiences, unity is strengthened, empowering individuals to contribute positively to their communities and create a more inclusive and interconnected world.

I'm honored and humbled by the effect our friendship and working relationship have had on the varied fashion and faith communities. Yet, I'm more excited for what's next!

Photo courtesy of Mana Fashion Services
Designer: Kate McGuire (Converted Closet)

Photo courtesy of Mana Fashion Services
Designer: Aviad Arik Herman

Photo courtesy of Mana Fashion Services
Designer: Melanie Brandon

Photo courtesy of Mana Fashion Services
Designer: Kate McGuire (Converted Closet)

Photo courtesy of Mana Fashion Services
Designer: Melanie Brandon

Photo courtesy of Shoshi Yegudayov

Photo courtesy of Shoshi Yegudayov

Photo courtesy of Formentera Swim

Designer: Valeria Krasavina
Photographer: Tato Gomez

Photographer: Iris Hyde
Tobi Rubinstein

אֵשֶׁת חַיִל

אֵשֶׁת חַיִל מִי יִמְצָא, וְרָחֹק מִפְּנִינִים מִכְרָהּ.
בָּטַח בָּהּ, לֵב בַּעְלָהּ; וְשָׁלָל, לֹא יֶחְסָר.
גְּמָלַתְהוּ טוֹב וְלֹא-רָע כֹּל, יְמֵי חַיֶּיהָ.
דָּרְשָׁה, צֶמֶר וּפִשְׁתִּים; וַתַּעַשׂ, בְּחֵפֶץ כַּפֶּיהָ.
הָיְתָה, כָּאֳנִיּוֹת סוֹחֵר; מִמֶּרְחָק, תָּבִיא לַחְמָהּ.
וַתָּקָם, בְּעוֹד לַיְלָה וַתִּתֵּן טֶרֶף לְבֵיתָהּ; וְחֹק, לְנַעֲרֹתֶיהָ.
זָמְמָה שָׂדֶה, וַתִּקָּחֵהוּ; מִפְּרִי כַפֶּיהָ, נָטְעָה כָּרֶם.
חָגְרָה בְעוֹז מָתְנֶיהָ; וַתְּאַמֵּץ, זְרוֹעֹתֶיהָ.
טָעֲמָה, כִּי-טוֹב סַחְרָהּ; לֹא-יִכְבֶּה בַלַּיְלָה נֵרָהּ.
יָדֶיהָ, שִׁלְּחָה בַכִּישׁוֹר; וְכַפֶּיהָ, תָּמְכוּ פָלֶךְ.
כַּפָּהּ, פָּרְשָׂה לֶעָנִי; וְיָדֶיהָ, שִׁלְּחָה לָאֶבְיוֹן.
לֹא-תִירָא לְבֵיתָהּ מִשָּׁלֶג: כִּי כָל-בֵּיתָהּ, לָבֻשׁ שָׁנִים.
מַרְבַדִּים עָשְׂתָה-לָּהּ; שֵׁשׁ וְאַרְגָּמָן לְבוּשָׁהּ.
נוֹדָע בַּשְּׁעָרִים בַּעְלָהּ; בְּשִׁבְתּוֹ, עִם-זִקְנֵי-אָרֶץ.
סָדִין עָשְׂתָה, וַתִּמְכֹּר; וַחֲגוֹר, נָתְנָה לַכְּנַעֲנִי.
עֹז-וְהָדָר לְבוּשָׁהּ; וַתִּשְׂחַק, לְיוֹם אַחֲרוֹן.
פִּיהָ, פָּתְחָה בְחָכְמָה; וְתוֹרַת חֶסֶד, עַל-לְשׁוֹנָהּ.
צוֹפִיָּה, הֲלִיכוֹת בֵּיתָהּ; וְלֶחֶם עַצְלוּת, לֹא תֹאכֵל.
קָמוּ בָנֶיהָ, וַיְאַשְּׁרוּהָ; בַּעְלָהּ, וַיְהַלְלָהּ.
רַבּוֹת בָּנוֹת, עָשׂוּ חָיִל; וְאַתְּ, עָלִית עַל-כֻּלָּנָה.
שֶׁקֶר הַחֵן, וְהֶבֶל הַיֹּפִי: אִשָּׁה יִרְאַת-יְהוָה, הִיא תִתְהַלָּל.
תְּנוּ-לָהּ, מִפְּרִי יָדֶיהָ; וִיהַלְלוּהָ בַשְּׁעָרִים מַעֲשֶׂיהָ.

Photo courtesy of Sharon Schurder

Styled by Zubaidah
Photographer: Najmah Nicole Abraham

Photo courtesy of St. Thomas University

Photo Credit: Mikael Aghal
Model: Veronica Collins

CHAPTER TWO

JEWELRY

"I also put a ring in your nostril, earrings in your ears and a beautiful crown on your head."

Ezekiel 16:12

Photo by Uriel Setareh

Alhambra's Jewels

Van Cleef & Arpels, the renowned French jeweler and watchmaker, has captured the hearts of connoisseurs and fashion enthusiasts worldwide with its exquisite creations. Among its remarkable offerings, the Alhambra collection's rounded four-leaf clover (ish) stands as an iconic symbol of timeless elegance and beauty. Its distinct design has become a status symbol among tastemakers worldwide. As for me, it's an average design that comes in too many choices with too little excitement. Inspired by the enchanting Alhambra palace in Granada, Spain, the collection was introduced in 1968, capturing the essence of Moorish architecture and its symbolic meaning to nature and craftsmanship. Having been to this Spanish region, I find that it is a very loose interpretation of the rich and horrific history of the Alhambra, the palace and fortress complex located in Granada, Andalusia, Spain. During the reign of the Nasrid dynasty in the 14th century, the Alhambra became a royal residence decorated with intricate Islamic art and architecture.

It is considered one of the finest examples of Islamic architecture in the world and has been designated a UNESCO World Heritage Site. The Lion Fountain, or Fuente de los Leones, is a notable feature of the Alhambra that is often associated with the Jewish community. The fountain is located in the Court of the Lions, which is one of the most famous and beautiful areas of the palace. The fountain features a large basin supported by twelve lions, which are said to symbolize the twelve tribes of Israel. Spanish Jew·ry played an important role in the cultural and intellectual life of Andalusia during the Islamic period, and many of the artists and architects who worked on the Alhambra were likely influenced by Jewish ideas and aesthetics.

Yet, if you care to know the history of the next chapter for the Jews of Spain in that region and all the others, get ready to rid yourself of those pretty bracelets and layers of necklaces.

On March 31, 1492, the Edicto De Granada, also known as The Alhambra Decree, an edict of expulsion, was issued by King Ferdinand and Queen Isabella. This meant that all Jews must leave Spain entirely by the end of July without return, on pain of death or being forcibly converted to Christianity. Hundreds of thousands surrendered their Judaism to the Church, demoralized and baptized. While 100,000 chose exile, leaving everything they owned behind to be confiscated by the very country they so richly contributed to for 900 years. This is well known as "The Spanish Inquisition".

Officially, at least, there were no Jews in Spain until 1869, when the Expulsion Edict was revoked. Sephardic Jews did not begin returning in appreciable numbers until the 1950s.

500 years later, King Juan Carlos and Queen Sophia finally apologized to the Jews on the anniversary of Columbus's first voyage to the New World, ironically funded by The Jews of Spain.

In all fairness to Van Cleef and Arpels, a French master jeweler, they aren't responsible for the historic references of their most popular collection. Their website boasts the wonderful origins of the brand, which started in Paris in 1895. It's the story of a marriage and a family-run partnership, with involvement up until today.

I also confess that I've visited Spain twice and found the country absolutely beautiful. I am unable to share what I admire more: Flamenco dancing costumes of ruffles and long fringed shawls or the art of the fan. Funny enough, one trip I took was a Passover program that offered extensive tours throughout the holiday vacation time.

So, you don't have to return the Alhambra long necklace in tiger eye and diamonds that you might have posted on Instagram or the mother-of-pearl enamel bracelet. I would just love it if they renamed it "The Spanish Collection".

Holy Gems

I could not have asked for a better brand to include in the jewelry chapter. It is the world's only jewelry inlaid with natural precious gems made by G-d, mined in His Holy land, Israel. After she showcased her jewelry designs in the Haute and Holy runway show with Mana Fashion Services, I sat down with her to have this conversation about her family and their brand's remarkable story.

Tobi, "How much faith was required to sustain the hopes of finding the treasure?"

Tali, "As a starting point, you need to understand that the entire existence and reality of our business is based on faith. Our project would not have started if it were not for the words of one of the most influential Jewish leaders of our generation - the Lubavitcher Rebbe. Only because of our father's belief that the Rebbe is G-d's messenger on earth, and his words are sacred truth - he chose to put all his money, efforts, and prestige on this adventure against all odds. And to your question, the amount of faith that was involved in driving and sustaining our project can be perceived mainly in view of the many difficulties we managed to overcome along the way: starting with the skepticism of Israeli geologists who did not believe in the scientific feasibility of the existence of a gem deposit in Israel in the absence of previous relevant research; through the difficulties posed by the Israeli authorities who did not know how to address the matter from a regulatory point of view; and ending with the precious stones market in Israel, which was not prepared for the impact of gems originating in Israel on the market.

To all of these, you can add the great difficulties of raising funds (23 years of investment-based exploration), the expectations of the partners, and above all, of course, the exploration and research activities, which are considered a "needle in a haystack". Despite all these difficulties and obstacles, we did not give up on the faith and the dream, and as you can see today, the results are amazing."

Tobi, "Do you believe that jewelry can be holy? If so, why"?

Tali, "Of course! We believe that it can be holy because that is how G-d saw it. The best example of this is the famous jewel in history known as the breastplate that was on the heart of the High Cohen in the holy Temple, for all its sacred meanings. So, it was G-d who decided that gems embedded in jewelry would be holy objects."

Tobi, "Can jewelry enhance the holiness of dressing up?"

Tali, "There is a famous saying of Rabbi Bachya, who authored the book 'Duties of the Hearts', who said that: "The emotions are affected by the actions." That basically means that a person's actions can affect his mood and his perception of himself. In fashion or clothing, this is usually reflected in a direct effect on the mind—clothing that conveys something or a certain color (which affects your state of mind). Even in Kabbalah (and in many scientific studies), it has been proven that colors can also affect the mind.

In the same way, we believe (although it is ultimately individual) that a piece of jewelry containing precious gems mined from the depths of the Holy Land can have an effect of holiness, which is expressed mainly in a sense of security arising from a sense of belonging. A kind of unbreakable connection with the most sacred source in the world."

Tobi, "Can you describe the woman (or man) that gravitates towards your brand?"

Tali, "People with a developed spiritual awareness will easily connect with our gems; people with historical awareness will find the excitement of wearing gems that were mined from the land on which all the greatest kings in human history walked; lovers of modern Israel will discover through these amazing gems the connection between Israel's past and future. And of course, those who are looking for uniqueness and rarity in general and are looking for a jewel that cannot be found anywhere else in the world."

Tobi, "What are your plans to spread the holy word about your gems and jewelry?"

Tali, "It is important for us to reveal our miraculous story to as many people as possible, which is a story about faith that can conquer everything. So, we continue to tell our story through the media and social networks. For those interested, we enable the purchase of our rare jewelry from anywhere in the world through our website at www.holy-gems.com. We also opened a new visitor center near the operational mining complex in Akko, Israel, where people can literally find the wonders for themselves. And in light of the demand, we are opening a boutique branch in Jerusalem, and with G-d's help soon, we will open branches in other cities in the world where there is an interested audience."

The holy gem story is a modern-day miracle that miraculously left me with nothing else to write.

Crowned

The coronation of King Charles and Queen Camilla was a momentous occasion steeped in centuries of tradition and heritage. As the next in line to the throne of England, Prince Charles took on the role of king with all of the associated power, prestige, and responsibility. To mark this momentous event, new coronation crowns were made for the couple, which replaced the ones previously in use.

The history of the coronation crowns was significant not only for the royal family but for the wider public as well, as it represented a continuation of a centuries-old tradition. The ceremony of coronation has been held in Westminster Abbey since 1066, when William the Conqueror was crowned as the first Norman king of England. The crowning of a new monarch has always been an event marked with pomp and ceremony, with the crowns serving as a symbol of the authority and responsibility that come with the role of king or queen.

The updated head ornaments, designed by master jeweler Harry Collins, were lighter and more comfortable to wear than their predecessors, which were heavy and cumbersome. The designs were intended to maintain the traditional elements of a royal crown while incorporating modern technology and design techniques.

The crowns featured many symbols and elements that paid tribute to the rich history of the royal family, including the use of precious gems and metals, intricate designs, and symbolic motifs. The designs also incorporated Celtic and Anglo-Saxon elements, reflecting the rich cultural heritage of the British Isles.

All this pageantry and jeweled golden crowns have a biblical past.

Rabbi Shimon said, "There are three crowns: the Crown of Torah, the Crown of Priesthood and the Crown of Royalty, but the Crown of a Good Name supersedes them all." (Ethics of the Fathers 4:1)

Three of the four primary objects in the holiest part of the Beis HaMikdash, the Holy Temple, had crowns that were seen as having golden rims: the Ark of the Covenant, the Golden Table, and the Golden Altar. The Ark, which contained the two tablets given by G-d to Moses, corresponds to the crown of the Torah. The Golden Altar, on which the kohanim, priests, offered the incense, corresponds to the crown of kehunah, priesthood. The Golden Table, on which the special bread was placed, corresponds to the crown of Malchus, or royalty.

Perhaps the most striking of the special garments worn by the Kohen Gadol (High Priest) was the tzitz. This was a gold plate tied around the forehead, engraved with the words "Holy to G-d." It was the priestly crown. Rav Kook explained that the tzitz, fashioned out of pure gold, reflected the loftiest spiritual riches, which gave the crown a holy meaning.

A crown sits on top of some Hebrew letters written on parchment. These decorated letters hide the Torah's secrets and hint at what has yet to be revealed. If you open the arc in most synagogues today, you will find the Torah scrolls dressed in embroidered velvets topped with the most elaborate crowns of silver or gold. The crown augments the Torah's status as an object associated with royalty and speaks to the centrality of the Torah in Jewish life. There is one exceptional piece in the Metropolitan Museum of Art that is a testimony to the goldsmith work of 18th-century Venice. This Torah crown is decorated with a miniature temple, a menorah, and the Tablets of the Law, the latter engraved in Hebrew with the Ten Commandments. Such rich embellishment is indicative of the wealth and influential status of the Jewish congregation in the Venetian city. Andrea Zambelli, the artist, is known to have made a wide range of ritual Judaica as well as religious silver for the local churches.

During these times, I think we all deserve a crown for keeping our sanity as we reign over our own kingdoms. We should strive to be crowned in love, peace, and understanding that the only real king is G-d.

"Crown of glory, and diadem of beauty." [Isaiah 28:5]

Iris at 102

Youth has been a universal source of admiration, fawning, and obsession for generations. Older women strive to look younger, and teenagers want to be older. All ages have too much Botox to even show any emotions at all. It's a cosmetic and plastic surgery "Hotel California". They check in but never leave, except for Iris Apfel, a lone fighter against the system and a self-proclaimed "geriatric starlet" at 102.

She is recognized for her "more is more, less is a bore" approach to accessorizing. Iris has become a social media sensation (with 2.7 million followers) in recent years, inspiring all generations.

Her 100th birthday celebration was a spectacular introduction to her H&M collaboration. She shared this recap during an interview with The Today Show:

"With something for everybody, young and old," as Apfel described it, the "playful" and "very happy" collection includes statement pieces like a billowing violet jacket made from tulle swirls, a floral print tiered maxi skirt with a matching blouse, and a yellow-and-purple lounge set with fringe detailing. There are also bright mini dresses, flowy kaftans, and a swimsuit that pays tribute to my 100th birthday."

The collection sold out worldwide in record time. If you are an 'Emily in Paris' fan, then you spotted the purple piece in season 3.

As I wrote in my last book, she has worn a lot of hats over the course of her 102 years, from businessperson to interior designer for nine presidents to model, brand ambassador, cover girl, and mega influencer. Her later-life "celebrity" has come largely from the fact that she adorns herself with miles of bangles, dramatic necklaces, bold colors, and large-framed eyewear. She's got her very own Barbie, movies, books, eyewear, and makeup line. Do you have her rugs yet?

She is one of fashion's most instantly recognizable tastemakers. The bespectacled New Yorker's popularity was once a rare exception to fashion's love of youth. However, things are changing in no small part due to her wit, taste, and smart advice.

I feel very blessed that she's become a friend and mentor. I look forward to our yearly preparations for BIJOUX Contemporary, a jewelry show founded and produced by Donna Schneier, my MamaDonna. I get to play in a treasure chest of Iris's personal baubles. I witnessed her sassiness and sophistication while assorting, selecting, and selling her jewels to the thousands of attendees at this highly successful annual event at The Boca Raton Museum of Art.

Iris and her two caretakers, Jennifer and Julie, are a trio that bring so much warmth and caring to everything that they do.

Jewish teachings consider old age a virtue and a blessing. Throughout the Torah, "old" in Hebrew is "zaken" which is synonymous with "wise". G-d commands us to respect the elderly because of the many trials and experiences that each additional year of life brings. It develops a wisdom that even the most accomplished young prodigy cannot equal.

"One can be any age if one is, so to speak, a figure of youth, all of which comes from a spirit of continual self-education." - Diana Vreeland

In Iris's case, it's going to take an army of younger generations to catch up to her. As for me, I can only wish to grow up to be just like her.

Snakes

Bulgari's snake icon is an emblematic symbol that has become synonymous with the brand's jewelry and watch collections. The Serpenti, an iconic motif, draws inspiration from the captivating allure and symbolism associated with snakes, not to mention the status of power and privilege. Bulgari incorporated the snake into their designs during the 1940s, when animal-inspired jewelry was fashionable. It slithered its way into being the most sought-after design for the acclaimed jewelry house until today. The snake's coils are often featured in necklaces, bracelets, rings, earrings, and watches with exquisite details and world-renowned craftsmanship. The collection has been adorned by notable personalities, celebrities, and fashion icons, solidifying its status as a highly coveted symbol of style. The brand has introduced new design elements, such as colorful enamel, innovative materials, and unexpected combinations, keeping the Serpenti icon fresh and captivating for contemporary audiences.

I cringe just a little when thinking of wearing a snake, although I have had my eye on a pink and white enamel snake bangle watch. It is bejeweled with diamonds and rubies set in Rose Gold and can be found at Sotheby's... just a slight hint to my husband.

Fashion finds design elements in snakes, but religion has something of another skin. In Judaism, the snake holds significant symbolic meaning, primarily based on its appearance in the story of Adam and Eve in the Book of Genesis. The snake is associated with temptation and terribly permanent change for mankind. In the Garden of Eden, the creature (although nothing like the modern-day snake) led Eve (she led Adam) to eat from the forbidden fruit of the Tree of Knowledge. This act led to the disobedience of G-d's commandment, which resulted in the loss of innocence. The snake is often seen as a representation of the inclination towards evil, known as the "yetzer Harah," and is quite dangerous on many levels. The Talmud states that a snake will bite a person or animal even when it has not thought of eating it (Ta'anit 8a). The Talmud equates it to a man who gossips about his fellow, though he receives no tangible pleasure from doing so. Interestingly, the Jewish Sages were especially concerned about snakes coming to drink water left uncovered overnight, leaving some of their venom in the water (Talmud Avodah Zarah 30). Some are still stringent regarding this today. The Sages also viewed snakes as typical "messengers" that G-d sends to punish the wicked.

Snakes have completely reversed sentiments in Hinduism, Buddhism, and Jainism, as they are considered holy. Hinduism believes that the serpents represent various concepts such as spiritual awakening, divine protection, fertility, rebirth, and the cosmic order. They are associated with Kundalini energy, serve as guardians, signify cyclical transformation, and embody the balance of the universe. However, Christianity and Islam agree with the biblical Jewish thoughts on the slithery subject.

Nearly every culture has worshipped, revered, or feared them. I don't believe there could be a more complex creature to get in contact with... except a golden version in diamonds wrapped around your wrist.

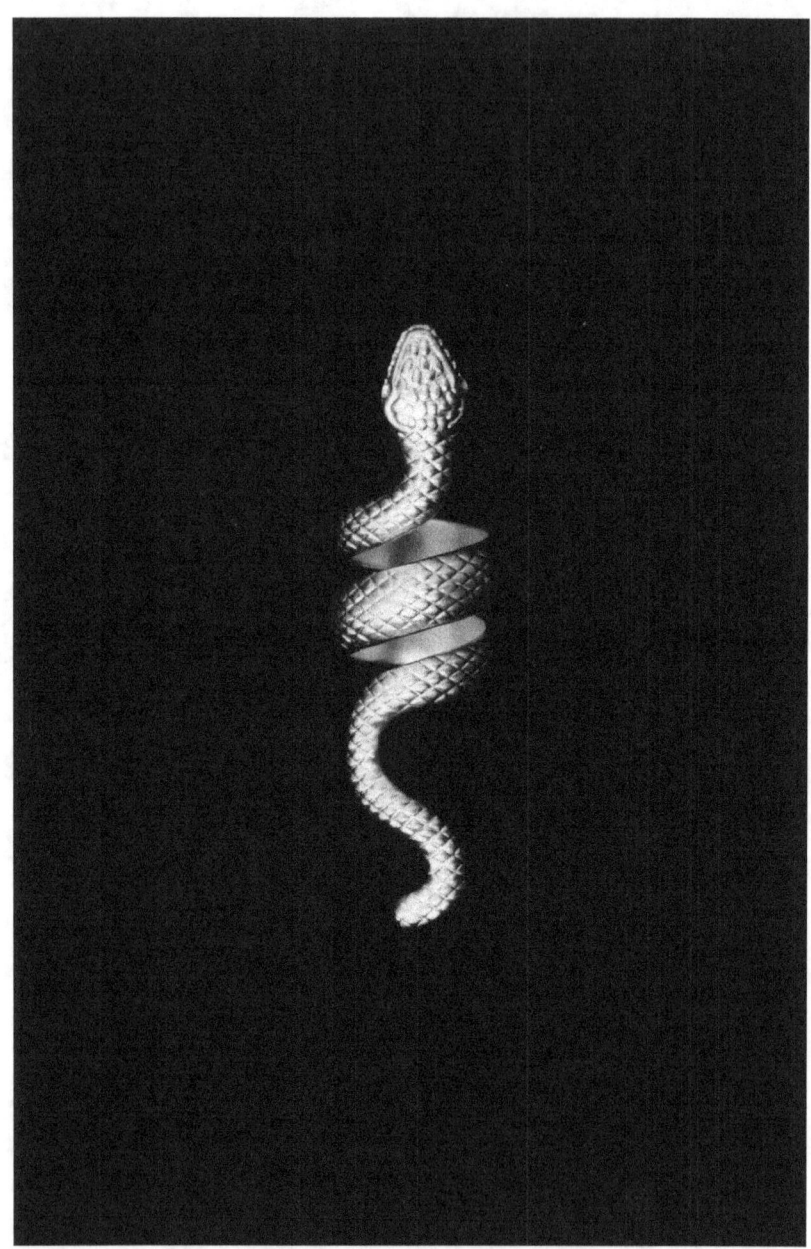

Photo courtesy of Gil Zohar

Alhambra

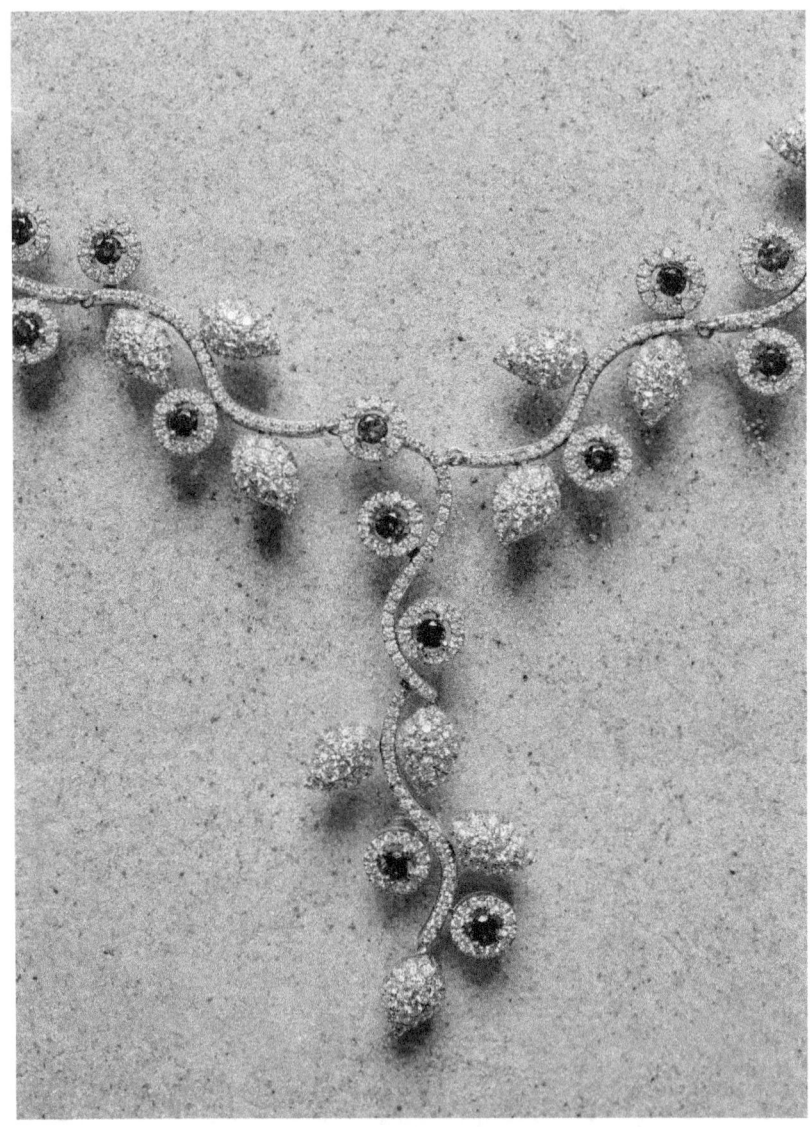

Photo courtesy of Holy gems

Photo courtesy of Holy Gems

Torah Crown Photo by Uriel Setareh

Photo by Iris Hyde

Iris Apfel

Photo courtesy of Bijoux Contemporary
Donna Schneier

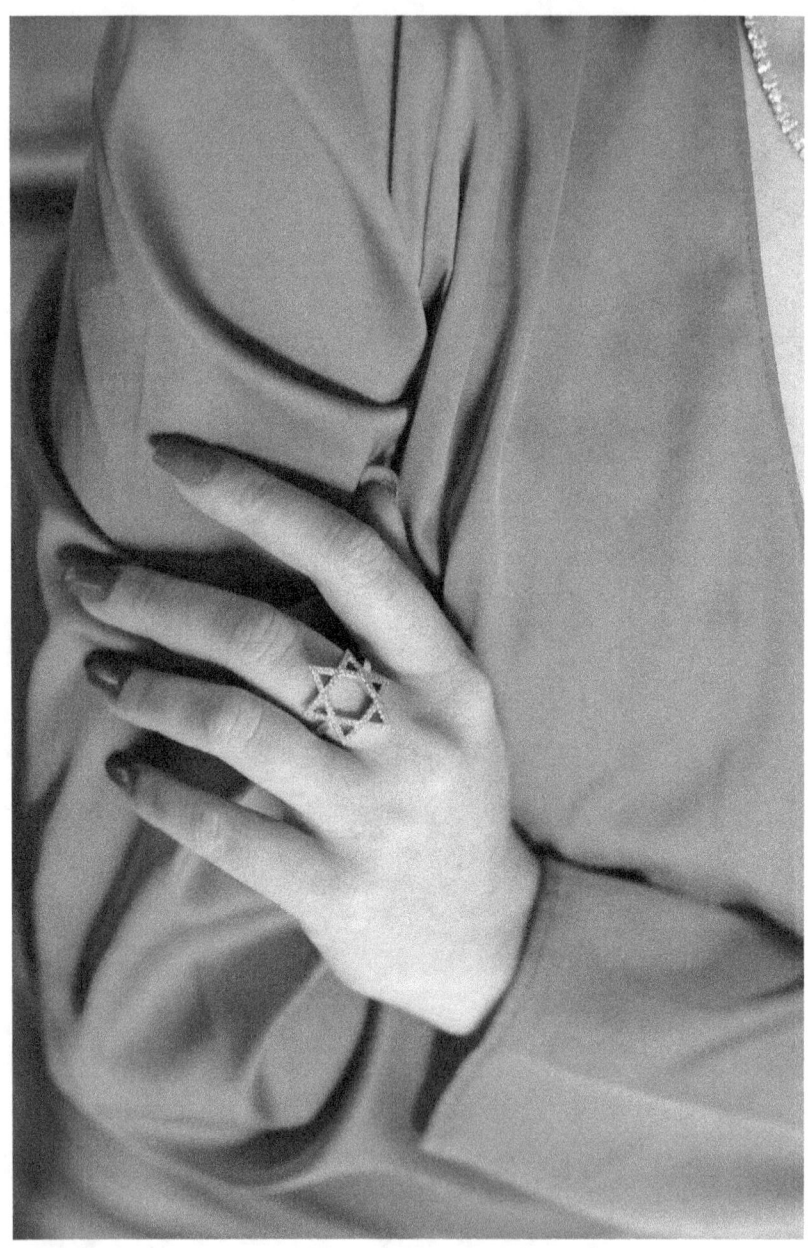

Jewelry by Ifat Oved

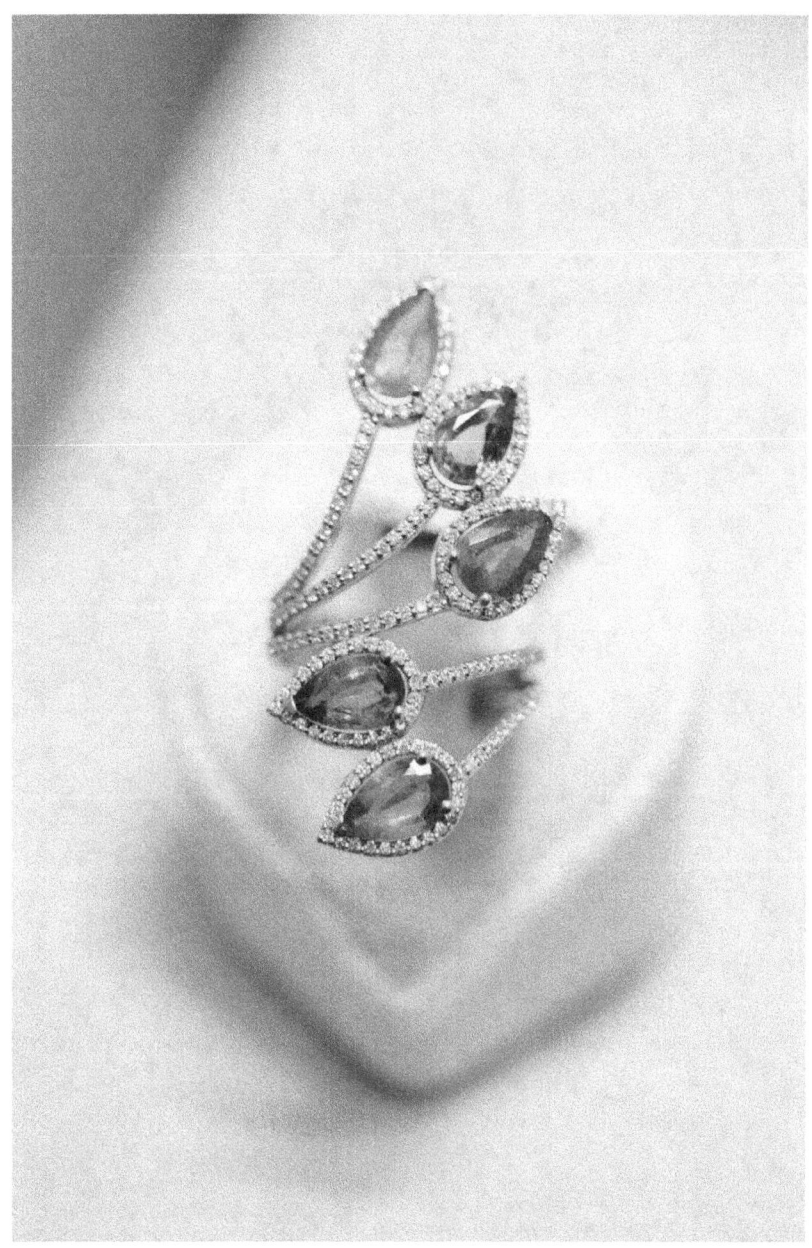

Jewelry by Ifat Oved

Photo courtesy of Iris Hyde
Earrings by Liat Ginzburg

Jewelry by Iris Apfel

CHAPTER THREE

BEAUTY & LIFESTYLE

"Which is the proper path for man to choose for himself? Whatever brings beauty to the person that does it and is beautiful to mankind."

Ethics of The Fathers (2:1)

Tobi Rubinstein

Mani Pedi

One of life's great pleasures and necessities is a mani-pedi. This is a magic duo of beauty services that transports one into a spa-like existence for at least an hour and a half. Those dangerously long painted canvases extending from your fingertips can be shaped pointy or square, almond or deadly weapon, shellac-ed or gelled, chrome or crimson, jeweled or jazzed. Our nails are the newest fashion accessory. Whether you follow Cardi B and Nails on 7 or Stars like Dua Lipa and Megan Thee Stallion, they have been rocking 3D nail art manicures for quite some time.

There are three superstars in nail artistry. Dawn Sterling is a New York-based nail artist whose handiwork was featured in the spring 2023 shows of The Row and Marni. Her favorite nail design is the pink and white manicure with added chrome. Betina Goldstein served as a nail artist for Chanel. Her nail craft extends to 3D designs of unexpected objects, making a classic nail pop. Kim Truong got a career boost from her relationship with the Kardashians. Her favorite design is hand-painted white flower petals over pearly glazed cream.

If you are a fan of manicures, you might be surprised that Jewish law has a thing or two to say about nail care. One would not naturally think that such a mundane activity could have spiritual ramifications, but it does.

For instance, traditional Jewish thought discourages cutting one's fingernails and toenails on the same day, as it is said to lead to forgetfulness. It does, however, encourage a person to cut their nails on Friday, in particular, as part of their Shabbat preparation. In the Talmud, it is written that three things were said about nails. "One who buries them is [deemed] righteous. One who burns them is [considered] pious. One who throws them away is [regarded as] wicked. What is the reason? Lest a pregnant women pass over them and miscarry" (Talmud Moed Katan 18a).

The Kabbalah has its own manicure ritual in which you cut your nails in a preferred order, beginning with the left hand and trimming the ring finger, index finger, pinky, middle, and thumb. Switching to the right hand, one then trims the index, ring, thumb, middle, and pinky. This custom applies to fingernails only and is quite a dance for your fingers.

As per the Laws of Marriage Purity, during the monthly visit to the Mikveh (ritual bath), one is advised to clean up their nails as part of the cleansing process. The extent of stringency in the interpretation of the law about polish, gel, extensions, and length is entirely up to the various community standards.

During Havdalah (the closing ceremony of the Sabbath), we light candles and recite four blessings, including *borei me'orei ha'esh*, "Blessed are You ... who creates the lights of the flame," after which we look at our fingernails in the candlelight. The late Midrashic work Pirkei d'Rabbi Eliezer [8thcentury, ch. 20] mentions it, and R. Hai Gaon [d. 1038, Iraq] reports a charming reason for this is because fingernails are always growing, and looking at them is a good omen for a week of success [Responsa Shaarei Teshuvah 104].

Jewish Mysticism explains that The Torah states that when Adam and Eve sinned in the Garden of Eden and realized they were naked, G-d clothed them in /kutnot or, "garments of leather," to hide their shame. Midrashic interpreters enjoyed a little word play, swapped a letter alef for ayin, and said that up until they sinned, Adam and Eve wore kutnot or, "garments of light." "They were smooth as nail and radiant like pearls" [Bereshit Rabbah 20.12]. Adam's and Eve's original bodies were really made of keratin, the material we still have on our fingertips.

There is so much to explore about fingernails in religious practice, but I'm running late for my mani-pedi appointment!

Coffee and Babka

The Torah portion called "B'shalach" addresses the issue of the Egyptians punishments from G-d, which included their horses. They all drowned in the Red Sea after the Israelites safely passed through to the other side. This incident begs the question, If the horses were a part of the sin, they must also be a part of a good deed?

This morning I had my last coffee with Lady Cinnamon Babka, our beautiful Wheaton Terrier with furry hair that matched the crumble coating of a freshly baked cinnamon babka. Every morning for the last 11 and a half years, she permitted me to perform my first string of Mitzvot (good deeds) that started my day. This act dates back to being a little girl with my zaidy (grandfather) back in Brooklyn's East New York neighborhood. "Toba Leah, you must feed the dog before you eat in the morning because G-d commanded that," was his mantra as he handed Dukie, our wolf mix breed, his bowl of food, which consisted of Shabbos meal leftovers. I heard my zaidy's thoughtful voice every morning as the coffee brewed and I prepared Babka's mix of last night's leftovers and rice. Yet in her last few days, as she struggled with cancer and very sudden unforeseen complications, she settled only for a small chewing bone placed gently by her nose as our morning ritual.

Babka was given to me as a gift from my daughter Lola after Chedda, our first Wheaton Terrier, passed away. Fearing that I would feel lonely as an empty nester as she was leaving for college, she gifted me a little 4-month-old Wheaton female puppy. At first, I resented her, as her presence didn't allow me to properly mourn my last dog, who meant so much to me for nine years. Coupled with the fact that I had never owned a female dog, I found myself unwilling to warm up to her at all.

She was different, sensitive, and shy, as she hid under every surface she could find. Yet, it was becoming more apparent that she was hardly a puppy I could ignore, and slowly I fell in love with her unique heart-shaped face and playful bouncing. Just like Chedda, she became my sidekick for everything going on in my life, which included being my co-host, therapist, relationship couch, sous-chef, and wing girl.

Yet, with all those titles, the most outstanding was brought to life when I was diagnosed with my first set of medical challenges. Having her sleep with me in the downstairs den as I recovered from my hip replacement seemed like a very natural assignment for her. She quickly graduated to head of my nursing needs when I was side swiped with stage 4 cancer. The first round of chemotherapy (during COVID) was truly a horrifying and lonely experience that I will never forget; however, the sound of Babka screaming in the back seat of the car on the ride to Mount Sinai Hospital was a sound I had never heard. She was alerting everyone, including me, that she felt and anticipated my pain and fear of what was about to occur for the next two years. It was her alarm to the world that she knows, and she will be on duty for as long as it takes for me to heal. She certainly kept her word and policed every session and every day that it took for me to withstand and recuperate by laying her body across mine as if to absorb and try to control the pain and all the side effects.

My family credits Babka with a big part of my recovery as a badge of honor for her services during my personal war with disease. She celebrated my recovery and even attended my Feast of Gratitude when it was finally concluded.

She was our mitzvah dog in various ways, as my husband took her to visit his elderly mom almost every day till she passed at 102. Shabbos and all the culinary delights were noted and appreciated by her as she did a special dance during Friday night kiddish, patiently waited for the brisket to be sliced, and hoped to get a good portion of my Moroccan salmon.

Are dogs G-d's favorite creature? Certainly a favored one, as He blessed them during the exit plan of Egypt as they didn't bark or interfere with the last plague. Nor did they make a sound while millions of Jews exited. Their Hebrew name is Caleb, meaning "like my heart" which is certainly a perfect description on so many levels.

Babka passed away after the last morning mitzvah we had together. I held her till her last breath while thanking Hashem for giving me such a precious gift. I knew that one day He would want her returned.

Perfume

Chanel No. 5 and Dior's Miss Dior are two of the most iconic fragrances in the world, loved and admired for their unique scent profiles and timeless appeal. Launched in 1921, Chanel No. 5 was created by perfumer Ernest Beaux for Coco Chanel and quickly became known for its complex floral-aldehydic composition. This fragrance revolutionized the industry, setting a new standard for luxury and sophistication. To this day, Chanel No. 5 remains highly popular, with a loyal following and a place in the fragrance hall of fame.

Miss Dior, on the other hand, was introduced in 1947 and marked Christian Dior's first foray into the fragrance world. Created by perfumer Jean Carles, Miss Dior is known for its elegant and feminine character, combining floral and chypre notes. Over the years, this iconic fragrance has been reformulated and reimagined with various flankers and editions. Despite these changes, Miss Dior has maintained its relevance and appeal among fragrance enthusiasts, solidifying its status as one of the all-time greats. Interestingly enough, Dior named this perfume after his sister, Catherine Dior. During WW2, she was a part of the French Resistance, where she was tortured with a death march and placed as a prisoner in a women's concentration camp.

Baccarat, a renowned crystal manufacturer, has ventured into the fragrance industry with its own perfume line. Launched in 2014, Baccarat Rouge 540 is the product of a collaboration between Baccarat and perfumer Francis Kurkdjian. This luxurious and distinctive scent features a blend of floral, woody, and amber notes. Despite being relatively new to the perfume scene, Baccarat

Rouge 540 has garnered attention for its unique composition and association with the prestigious Baccarat brand. It has gained a devoted following, particularly among fragrance connoisseurs and collectors who appreciate its exclusivity and niche appeal. While Chanel No. 5 and Miss Dior have a long-standing legacy and widespread recognition, Baccarat perfume has managed to carve out its own space in the fragrance industry.

Perfume holds significant symbolic and ritualistic importance in Judaism and other religions. Fragrance is a Holy scent.

The kettoret refers to the sacred incense blend prescribed by G-d in the Torah for use in the Tabernacle and later in the Holy Temple in Jerusalem. It consisted of a specific combination of aromatic ingredients, including frankincense, myrrh, galbanum, and other spices. The kettoret was prepared and offered by the high priest on the golden altar twice daily, representing a sweet offering to G-d. Its fragrance was intended to create a pleasant aroma within the sanctuary, symbolizing the spiritual elevation of prayers and offerings to G-d.

The ritual of the Havdalah service marks the end of Shabbat and the transition into the new week. As part of the Havdalah ceremony, various symbolic elements are used, including the b'samim, or spices. The b'samim, which means "fragrance" in Hebrew, are a collection of aromatic spices. They are chosen for their pleasant and distinctive scents. The purpose of the b'samim is to awaken the senses, particularly the sense of smell, after the spiritual rest of Shabbat. Common spices used as b'samim include cloves, cinnamon, nutmeg, cardamom, and other fragrant herbs or spices. They are typically held in a special container called a

B'samia box or spice container. During the Havdalah ceremony, the person leading the ritual passes the box for everyone to smell, accompanied by a blessing expressing gratitude for the fragrant spices and the separation between the sacred and the mundane.

These Judaic and Biblical practices have impacted other religions. The Roman Catholic Church burns frankincense during mass to create a time of solemnity, enhance holiness, and signify the presence of G-d. Similarly, the Eastern Orthodox Church uses fragrant herbs such as myrrh, cinnamon, saffron, and frankincense during worship services to symbolize the rising prayers of the faithful.

Yes, a spritz of Baccarat has a luxurious smell. A bottle of Chanel No. 5 is a classic on your vanity table. Miss Dior is a feminine eau de parfum; however, the notes blended by G-d make him the master perfumer.

Menorah

The menorah is a symbol of the Jewish holiday of Chanukah, which commemorates the rededication of the Holy Temple in Jerusalem after it was reclaimed from the Greeks in the second century BCE. During this eight-day holiday, Jews light candles on a special candelabrum called a menorah, adding one candle each night until all eight are lit on the final night. The menorah represents the miracle of the oil, where a small amount that was only enough to last for one day ended up lasting for eight days.

After the Chanukah holiday, it is customary to put away the menorah until the following year. However, before doing so, many people have the tradition of writing down their wishes or prayers on a small piece of paper and tucking it away with the menorah. This practice is based on the idea that the menorah represents not only the miracle of the oil but also the inner light that each of us possesses.

This ritual acknowledges that we have the power to cultivate and nourish our own inner light. It is a reminder that even in the darkest times, we can find our own sources of light and hope with G-d.

Additionally, the act of writing down our wishes can be a powerful way of clarifying our intentions and desires. It allows us to focus our thoughts and energies on what truly matters to us and to articulate our dreams and aspirations in a concrete way. By writing down our wishes and tucking them away with the menorah, we are creating a tangible reminder of our goals and a symbol of the light that we carry within us.

As painful as it is to share, I need to give my personal examples. In year 5781 (2021), I put the following under my Menorah:

"Hashem (G-d),

Please take all this cancer out of me in the least painful and fastest way possible. I got your message of love this morning. Thank you for my Felipe and Lola, plus all the special people in my life. Please help all the sick in Am Yisrael. Please, Hashem, give me the strength to endure and write the book to help enlighten others. Please, please rid me of the cancer in my body."

Even though this was short and precise, this piece of paper held the depths of my desires. I wrote it, let it go, and left it in the hands of G-d. I trusted that whatever the outcome will be, G-d had my best interests in mind.

I haven't unveiled this year's version, as it's still safely tucked away under the protection of my menorah.

Wigs

I can't say that I always "covered my hair" as I went through different stages of my life. Frankly, when I was growing up, wigs were not a focal point of a Jewish woman's wardrobe. Most of my friend's mothers only wore hats to synagogue services, and that was the extent of their hair coverings. My appreciation of hair, or the lack of it, came with menopause coupled with chemotherapy. Those two life-altering episodes madly frolicked in my follicles.

Wigs span many cultures and genders. Beyoncé wears a great one; Cardi B has the best ones; and every TV anchor hides one. They range in price from $39 to a 6-month mortgage payment. Wigs can change you, break you, disguise you, heal you, and enhance you, but in Judaism, they just might endear you to G-d. Also known as "sheitels" in Yiddish, wigs have become a notable aspect of Jewish practices among married Orthodox women.

The tradition dates back to ancient times. In Jewish law, it is considered a modesty requirement if you are married that your natural hair not be on public display.

It wasn't until the 16th century that Jewish women in Italy popularized the idea of wearing a wig as a covering, which actually ended up causing a huge debate among rabbis, who both condemned and condoned the practice of wearing them. However, as social norms and fashion evolved, wigs gradually became a popular alternative, offering a more natural appearance. The subject of wigs as religiously proper hair coverings is still surrounded by controversy or criticism from Rabbis that claim "they look better than real hair," which results in an attractiveness that is more difficult for them to navigate. The Lubavitch/Chabad women are assured that The Rebbe (ZL) had no objection at all to wigs that enhanced a woman's appearance. On the contrary, he encouraged women to take advantage of their availability. "Even today, there lingers in many minds the erroneous notion that hair covering is meant to detract from a married woman's attractiveness," says Chabad.org. This flies against the other Chassidic movements that wear shorter, far less attractive versions.

Historically, the human-hair wig first appeared in ancient times but virtually disappeared after the fall of Rome in 476 CE. It reappeared in the last five centuries because of King Louis XIII of France, who, on account of his concern about his own personal male pattern baldness, advanced the technology that has evolved into the modern SHEITEL.

The Egyptians wore wigs to protect against the hot sun. They attached the wigs to their heads using beeswax and resin. The Assyrians, Greeks, and Romans also used wigs. The term WIG, by the way, is short for PERIWIG.

Today, the highly sophisticated, proliferating wig industry offers truly beautiful options in synthetic and human hair alike. As in fashion, wigs have "mass market" brands and "designer" brands, but Haute Couture belongs to the brand called Dini.

Dini Wigs exude passion, creativity, and flawless fashion. With her artistic flair and profound understanding of hair, the founder, Dini, has revolutionized the wig industry. I've paid close attention to her social media, as I find that she has a playful approach to the serious situation of finding and fitting a wig. Often times, it's a very personal experience that requires a lot of handholding and patience. Some clients want to enhance their already beautiful faces, and some want to recapture what they once had. This includes mothers overseeing their daughter's first purchase with complete joy. On the other end of the spectrum, there is someone like myself who needed a wig to survive chemotherapy sessions while remaining sane. I still play with my turquoise and gray short bob that I rocked one seder three years ago.

I contacted Dini while she was packing for her trip to her Paris store's grand opening. I knew that these questions would speak to her, as she already lives a life that seamlessly combines faith and fashion.

Tobi, "Dini, do you believe that your craft as a wig maker is a G-d given talent?"

Dini, "Of course! I believe everything is from G-d. I feel so fortunate to be able to do what I love every day, and I thank him for showing me the way. As a young girl, I always loved hair (yes, I was that friend who everyone asked to cut and style their hair). From a young age, I already loved playing with wigs. I would go with my mother to her sheitel macher and my mother would just leave me there because I just didn't want to leave till closing. G-d blessed me with parents who allowed me to take my first wig course at age 16, and that's when I fell in love with wigs in particular! There's something about wigs that is truly transformational. Yes, a good hair cut is valued, but it's so fun to give one person five different looks."

Tobi, "Do you agree that a great wig could give you more faith in yourself while adhering to a faith-based law?"

Dini, "I love the way this question is phrased, and the answer is totally! A great wig can give someone more confidence. When you look better, you feel better, so you do better. I believe that when you're confident in yourself, you're better able to serve Hashem. There's also a big concept in Judaism about beautifying the mitzvos—what better way to do that than ensuring what you wear every day makes you feel beautiful and confident?"

Tobi, "Can you give an example of your best transformation? Where have you witnessed a woman almost come alive with a beautiful wig?"

Dini, "This might sound funny, but it happens a lot more than you think! It happens with cancer patients who come in with no hair. It happens to women who decide to cover their hair for the first time. It even happens to women who have been covering their hair for years with scarves and hats and decide to go the wig route. It's very meaningful to watch a woman put on that wig for the first time and just glow. I constantly hear, "Wow, I look like me again." What can be better than giving someone a sense of their identity back?

One story I can think of that is particularly meaningful is when I had a client give me a $100 bill. Mind you, I don't deal with payments or accounting, so I am quite confused. However, she told me that her mother was the Lubavitcher Rebbe's cardiologist's seamstress. Her family weren't practicing Jews; however, she had gone to the rebbe for a blessing and saved the bill. She said to herself that she would save it for something meaningful. When her daughter was diagnosed with cancer, she knew she wanted to give it to us—a Jewish-owned wig company that was helping her daughter. And let me tell you, that wig totally transformed the daughter and helped her feel more hopeful going into treatment. It was emotional for everyone."

All of her answers spoke to me on many levels, as she confirmed what I had already thought about her. Since I'm not a Dini customer, this detachment allowed me the best assessment of Dini, the woman, and Dini, the business. As in most Jewish practices, there are many interpretations and opinions out there, probably enough to make your head spin. But if it's going to spin, do it with a Dini.

Eternal Relevance

"This clip is great! Thank you for sharing," was the text that Bernt Ullmann returned after I sent him my PowerPoint presentation for the Fashion Group International trend report event in Miami. Bernt is the most powerful licensing agent in the industry, going all the way back to the day we met at Phat Farm. He refers to himself as a Chief Brand Accelerator and has a star-studded client list that includes Jennifer Lopez, Nicki Minaj, and Adam Levine. His illustrious career goes back to the days of FUBU and the beginning of the hip-hop industry. He's a 6-billion-dollar man and a longtime friend.

What did I share? My new terminology for branding excellence is "Eternal Relevance". It is more than an icon, more than an evergreen, and more than a legend.

I came up with this term as I answered a student's question while teaching at the Sy Syms School of Business at Yeshiva University as a guest lecturer with professor and media star Ari Zoldan. "What do you wish to accomplish in 10 years with The House of Faith and Fashion?" was a perfectly suitable question, but one that I paused at. "Eternal Relevance" was the first thing that came out of my mouth, like a heavenly message for this branding graduate school class.

Eternal Relevance is a term that means remaining relevant in every decade with every age group across all spectrums. It means existing without an end, bigger and better than the term icon." When I was preparing for my talk at FGI (South Florida), I introduced the concept along with the appointment of the very first ambassador of Eternal Relevance, Barbie!

Barbie, although a mere toy, is more than just a plastic figurine. This iconic doll has been a source of fascination and controversy since her introduction in 1959. With her impeccably styled hair, sparkling outfits, and dreamy lifestyle, she has captured the hearts of millions of young girls worldwide.

Barbie's impeccable style has been a hallmark of her brand, setting her apart as a fashion icon. Her outfits, meticulously crafted to showcase the latest trends in fashion, have been a source of inspiration for young girls. From her cocktail dresses to her swimwear, she has set a high standard in fashion and sophistication, making her the perfect role model for young girls who aspire to be elegant and stylish.

Moreover, Barbie has been credited with empowering girls and promoting gender equality. Her vast range of professions, from teacher to doctor, shows young girls that they can choose any career they wish. Barbie has encouraged young girls to aim high, work hard, and excel in their respective fields. And now she's even a real-life (sort of) Movie Star, as this past summer made you see pink!

Her Jewish roots make her even more interesting. Ruth Handler was born in 1916 in Denver, a descendant of Jewish immigrants. She created Barbie in 1959 after observing her daughter, Barbara, playing with paper dolls and imagining them in grown-up roles. She recognized that there was a gap in the toy market for a three-dimensional doll that represented an adult woman. At the time, most dolls were baby or toddler-sized, and Handler saw an opportunity to create a doll that reflected the aspirations of young girls who desired to be sophisticated adults. With her husband Elliot and business partner Harold Mattson, Handler developed Barbie, named after her daughter, and launched her at the New York Toy Fair. The sleekly designed doll, with its blonde hair and fashionable wardrobe, was an immediate success and became a cultural icon for generations of young girls, and I was certainly one of them!

Barbie's future looks bright pink as the movie moves her past being a play doll and into a state of mind. She is not playing around with her status and impact; however, at this point in time (albeit a pink point), I believe G-d is the Supreme Ambassador of Eternal Relevance. G-d is eternal and relevant in all aspects of life, before, during, and the afterlife, which is far greater than the Malibu Barbie Dream House!

Red Lipstick

I stared at my phone in pure disbelief at the text message that I just received. It was from the assistant of this generation's most conservative, religiously right-wing Rabbinical lecturer. He has millions of views and thousands of followers. He's truly the last person I thought would ever contact me requesting an interview because he is so critical of Jewish women, their clothes, and their red lipstick! I was instructed to contact him at a certain time and date, which I gladly did. I started the conversation with a humorous warning: "Do you know what my book is about? I just want to tell you that I'm not taking off my high heels or my red lipstick!" We actually both started laughing, knowing that perhaps this interview might not come to fruition as expected. We agreed to disagree with mutual respect, which is quite out of the ordinary for a Rabbi of such religious adherence. I found his behavior to be most honorable, and I respect him more for how he handled the situation.

I still listen to his "repent or else" fire and brimstone lectures and continue to filter out the parts that make my makeup melt. It reminds me of my late zaidy, Mechel Roth, who took me to the Christmas show at Radio City Music Hall when I was just a little girl. When Santa arrived at the end of the gloriously magical, larger-than-life holiday show, my zaidy leaned over and whispered in my ear, "Toba Leah, ignore this part; it's not for you!" I learned how to apply his method of discernment to the Nutcracker Ballet, the Rockefeller Christmas Tree, and every tempting Santa Land installment in every mall around the world.

Luckily, I've been a blank canvas for so many talented makeup artists who ran amouk on me with shadows, brushes, bronzers, contouring, and smoky eyes. Those are all tricks and the language of the trade. Makeup, especially lipstick, has a special place in most women's hearts, dressers, and bathroom countertops.

Jewish businesspeople have been peddling lipstick for years; among them are Helena Rubinstein, Estée Lauder, and the Revson brothers. This practice continues with Bobbi Brown and Charlotte Tilbury.

Aside from its cosmetic enhancement, history has shown that lipstick can be a shimmer of life. British Lieutenant Colonel Mervin W. Gonin, commander of the 11th Light Field Ambulance, R.A.M.C., was among the first British soldiers to liberate Bergen-Belsen in 1945. In his diary, he gave a more graphic description of the effect of the lipstick:

"It was shortly after the British Red Cross arrived, though it may have no connection, that a very large quantity of lipstick arrived. This was not at all what we men wanted, we were screaming for hundreds and thousands of other things, and I don't know who asked for lipstick. I wish so much that I could discover who did it, it was the action of genius, sheer unadulterated brilliance. I believe nothing did more for these internees than the lipstick. Women lay in bed with no sheets and no nightie but with scarlet red lips, you saw them wandering around about with nothing but a blanket over their shoulders, but with scarlet red lips. I saw a woman dead on the postmortem table and clutched in her hand was a piece of lipstick. At last, someone had done something to make them individuals again, they were someone, no longer merely the number tattooed on their arm. At last, they could take an interest in their appearance. That lipstick started to give them back their humanity.»

The United States Holocaust Memorial Museum has the metal lipstick tube belonging to 21-year-old Masha Wolpe that she kept in a handmade burlap pouch while a prisoner at Stutthof concentration camp from July 1944 to April 1945. It also has the lipstick case carried by Irena Ehrlich vel Sluszny when she walked from Berlin to Warsaw in 1945 in search of her family.

Laura Geller, makeup mogul and QVC and HSN superstar, has been a friend for almost thirty years. Her signature line, Laura Geller Cosmetics, is one of the top-selling brands in the US and beyond. She's a favorite among A-List celebrities who cherish her honesty, practicality, charm, and great price points. After we did an Instagram live together about surviving cancer and beauty standards, I asked her a few questions.

Tobi, "Do you think your talent for makeup G-d given?"

Laura, "From a young age, I knew that going into the Makeup industry would be healing for myself and healing for the people I got to touch. I do believe I was chosen to forge this path in the beauty industry."

Tobi, "Can makeup enhance a woman's faith?"

Laura, "I think when a woman feels more confident in how she looks on the outside, that translates to how she feels about herself and her faith on the inside."

Tobi, "Why has makeup always remained fashionable?"

Laura, "It has always been a part of being fashion-forward. Most of the looks that are created in makeup are dictated by fashion trends."

Tobi, "Please share some personal examples of how being made up has helped you through a difficult situation."

Laura, "I have faced many adversities in life and in my career, for example, the loss of my mother and sister within a year of each other. Having to put my best face forward as a television personality, applying my makeup was not only comforting, but gave me strength to carry on."

Tobi, "How has faith appeared in your life and business?"

Laura, "Being a proud Jewish woman, I know there are not many of us in the world. It is my hope to inspire the next generation of men and women from all faiths and backgrounds, no matter how much the odds are stacked against them, to believe in their convictions, follow their dreams, and make a change for the better. And for that, I hope that I have done a small part in inspiring the next generation."

And of course...

Tobi, "What's your favorite shade of lipstick?"

Laura, "The colors of sunsets. On the day that both my mother and sister passed, this was what the sky looked like. It was peaceful and hopeful."

Obviously, lipstick is more than a stick of color. As Poppy King said so well, "Lipstick is a mind-altering substance. I think it's been miscast as cosmetic. It's so much more."

Photo courtesy of Dini Wigs

Photo courtesy of Dini Wigs

Photo courtesy of Elizabeth Sutton

Photo courtesy of Elizabeth Sutton

Babka

Photo courtesy of Laura Geller

Photo courtesy of Laura Geller

Photo courtesy of Laura Geller

Photo courtesy of Mana Fashion Services
Make up & hair by John Henry Edington III

CHAPTER FOUR

INFLUENCERS

"Power works by division, influence by multiplication."
Rabbi Lord Jonathan Sacks (ZL)

Talya

If you scroll through Instagram and try not to be bored with the assorted influencers that are doing and wearing the exact same things, then it's finally time for you to follow Talya. She brings back the color, the funk, and the fantastic fusion of faith and fashion.

"Talya Bendel is a two-time New York Times best-dressed and New York Times best-dressed For Parties 2022, Wardrobe stylist/Costumer for Film, Television and Editorial from NY/NJ. Her experience in these industries has led her to working with and for Christian Siriano, Netflix, Bazaar Vietnam, The Teletubbies and more with features in The New York Times, Refinery29, Voyage Jacksonville among others. Her main passion being creating magic from nothing and working with and empowering people helping them feel amazing in what they wear, whatever the occasion, is and always has been her goal."

Asking her these questions was just a natural way to get to know more about her life, career, and terribly courageous use of patterns and sparkles.

Tobi, "Becoming a fashion renegade takes courage; would you say that it took faith in yourself to express yourself? Please share that experience."

Talya, "I can definitely understand how I can be seen as a fashion renegade. The way I dress is far from mainstream, but if the way I dress became mainstream, I'd still dress the way I do. It's not about being different from other people or rebelling against an idea; it's more that I needed to find options that suited me that just weren't available until I found, created, or styled it myself. It's probably hard to understand how I can feel so comfortable wearing what I do without caring what others think, but I feel blessed that I just don't. That and the fact that I can't wear something I don't absolutely love, and the things I love are usually more "out of the box" than most would choose. I feel lucky to naturally do what works for me, and that translates to belief in myself enough and faith in myself to just do it."

Tobi, "Do you think that your talents are G-d given?"

Talya, "Yes. That being said, talent and skill are two different things. You are born with talents, but you can also build on them. The inclination at first is I believe G-d given. How much that grows depends on you. I was born with a great voice, but I was not born knowing how to sew a dress."

Tobi, "How do faith and your practices of faith weave into your world of fashion?"

Talya, "Being a modern Orthodox Jew means many things to many people. In my personal orthodoxy, it means adherence to Shabbat in levels that mean no use of electric items, travel, working, among other things. That and being in the fashion industry have not always aligned. While working for Christian Siriano, every Fashion week was bittersweet. The shows were always on Saturdays. Which meant I could never go. Imagine working as part of the production team for a Broadway play and never getting to watch it. It was fashion torture, and to be honest, pretty rough. At least I got to go to the parties, and Lord knows I love those. The main thing is that no matter what, I don't sacrifice my Judaism or my practice for anything that isn't absolutely necessary or life-threatening. My Judaism and practices are the core foundations of my life. Regardless of what happens in the fashion world, I don't sacrifice that."

Tobi, "Often, you channel Joseph's colorful coat in your fashion choices; do you agree? If so, what's your favorite one, and where did you wear it to?"

Talya, "I DEFINITELY agree. I love that comparison. I often wear many colors in one look. I am honestly so curious about what Joseph's dream coat actually looked like. That and the chosen (bejeweled breast plate used for the holy temple). One of my all-time favorite looks I've worn ended up on a New York Times best-dressed list. It was a combination of thrift in a graphic Harry Potter tee shirt under a mesh rainbow sparkly top. The sparkly top could easily be a variation of Joseph's dream coat in mesh shirt form. I wore it with a full black flared skirt and sparkly stilettos with a pink Barbie bag, so you can imagine it was colorful! I also wore it with a white root purple hair wig. You know, to add to the drama. I wore it for Saks and Bergdorf's fashion week kickoff parties, and it is my current all-time favorite look. One regret was that I had a staff that I was going to wear it with, but my party mates vehemently declined the idea. For good reason, as it probably would've been confiscated since it was pointy and maybe borderline cosplay. Regret it still, though slightly."

Tobi, "How does your Jewish faith impact your fashion practices?"

Talya, "Growing up religious, I did not have access to the clothing I wanted to wear. A. Because I had certain guidelines as to what I was allowed to wear, i.e., no pants, short sleeves, over the knee, or collarbone showing (common religious orthodox practice but not universal), B. My parents weren't buying me the styles I would've preferred because of price and availability, and that's only if the garment fell under the guidelines of A. And C., What I really wanted to wear didn't even exist at the time. Growing up with that hunger for my true expression and not being fulfilled with my aesthetic was the fire that pushed me to seek and create something different. Not different from everyone else, just different than the options in front of me while still, for the most part, sticking to my original guidelines. The way I dress changes every day, but the roots of my upbringing have not left me. I'm one of those people who believes everyone is brought into this world and into the environment, they were brought into for a reason. No matter where or who. Everyone has a purpose, and there is no one way to be. Even though I believe in my religious practices and that I am exactly where I'm supposed to be, that does not mean that they are meant for or good for everyone else."

Tobi, "Does modesty play a role?"

Talya, "Modesty has been a subject in my life since birth and has had major influences on my sartorial choices. For some, it is cut and dry, and for others, it is an enigma. It can be everything and anything if you are willing to see past a singular view. For me, as I understand it. There are times when I am modest, and there are times when I am not. I don't think modesty is in my nature in some ways, but in others, there are lines I would never cross. While also understanding that everyone has different lines. I am of the belief that if you are a good person who seeks to do no harm and, if possible, help regardless of what you look like or wear, that's a modest person. Breaking modesty down to seams versus how you appear is where the lines get crossed. Pun absolutely intended."

Tobi, "As your outfits are usually a burst of expression, has your faith held you back or propelled you to express yourself?"

Talya, "Thank you! My faith has definitely propelled me because I have had to work extra hard to get to a place where I don't have to sacrifice my style. It could also be why I got a degree in fashion design. My father always used to say I'm wearing "a schmatta on a schmatta," Schmatta meaning rag, because of the way I would layer my looks as a kid with pieces on pieces till I achieved what I was going for. As for bursts of expression through dress, that is very apropos to me because sometimes how I'm feeling leans into my look choices, and sometimes my look choices lean into how I'm feeling."

Tobi, "If you could compose a prayer through an outfit, what might that look like?"

Talya, "Great question! It may look a little like this,

From top to bottom

From head to toe

Let this look keep me safe.

Wherever we go"

She's Talya, as I have affectionately named the fashion renegade. Her voice pushes the creative process into spaces and places that wake up all your senses.

Good News

The power of positive news cannot be underestimated, for it has the ability to inspire and uplift even in the darkest of times. In a world where the constant barrage of negative news can leave one feeling hopeless and overwhelmed, a ray of hope and positivity can make all the difference. Good News reminds us that despite life's challenges and difficulties, there are always reasons to maintain a sense of hope and optimism. The power of positive news can also be seen in how it can change people's perspectives, helping them to see the world in a different light.

Last fall, I met the princess of good news, Halve Bouzo, the co-founder and host of YALLA Productions, an Arabic news outlet focusing on good news. She and her team hosted and broadcast the Haute and Holy panel talks on modest fashion in the Muslim, Jewish, and Christian communities. Prior to co-founding YALLA, Hayvi was a seasoned journalist having served as Washington bureau chief of Orient News, where she analyzed complex, highly nuanced regional political perspectives and reported the daily news. She created and hosted The Axis, a highly rated political TV show focused on U.S. policy towards the Middle East. The Axis was broadcast in more than 60 countries and viewed by millions in Europe and the Middle East. Someone with those qualifications could easily have worked for mainstream media outlets such as CNN or FOX. The fact that she paved her own path with the very popular YALLA shows her courage and willingness to convey the good news.

I asked Hayvi these questions as I knew her sensitivity, respect, and knowledge with regard to the combined topics of faith and fashion.

Tobi, "Do you find that "faith and fashion," as a combination, have a place in mainstream media where sensationalism is always desired?"

Hayvi, "Absolutely, in my opinion, faith and the belief in the One Divine, Higher Power in the Universe, is built into our DNA as a species. Using that essential part of us as an inspiration for creativity, art, and beautifying the world is an ultimate expression of the Divine. Fashion is an important form of creativity, self-expression, and the celebration of one's beliefs and culture. Turning both faith and fashion into a brand speaks to the hearts and souls of millions around the world, and I believe that there is not only a big market for it but that there is a hunger for it as well."

Tobi, "Are you finding that modesty practices are becoming more visible?"

Hayvi, "In the age of the internet and social media, everything has become a lot more visible, and individualism has become more prominent across the world. This includes modesty practices and modest fashion. People feel freer to express their own beliefs and values in the digital world. Yet, I think that there is still a lot of room for this genre to grow. Utilizing both digital and traditional media to accomplish this objective is the way to go."

Tobi, "How do you view the commonality of religious observance within dress with Muslim and Jewish faiths?"

Hayvi, "Modesty in dress that includes covering certain parts of the body is a part of both Jewish and Muslim laws and traditions. Yet, all women want to look and feel beautiful. In my opinion, there is no contradiction between looking beautiful, stylish, and fashionable and dressing modestly. This is where the power of the faith and fashion genre comes into play."

Tobi, "Your focus is on "good news" between faiths; can you share the best one that focuses on fashion?"

Hayvi, "Fashion shows and trends are usually a happy and positive topic. Also, generally, women and men from every background, religious belief, and ethnicity care about fashion and want to look their best. Yet, the concept of celebrating different faiths with fashion is an untapped, grand avenue for highlighting and sharing one's religion, culture, and tradition. We, at the Yalla show, want to promote this celebration of both uniqueness and commonalities across different religions and cultures to advance people to people's coexistence and peace in the Middle East, North Africa, and beyond."

Tobi, "Where do you see the most growth in bringing faiths together? Is the media part of that growth?"

Hayvi, "I do see a growth in bringing faiths and people together. An important example of this is the Abraham Accords Peace agreement between Israel and Arab countries. In the context of media coverage, this positive change is a bit more evident on social media—still not nearly enough—however hasn't yet translated to traditional media. At least not in the way that a broad, meaningful change is now in the making. As a broadcast journalist and an advocate for peace between the people, I do see the clear discrepancy in this area. This is why I believe that creating different platforms, movies, and shows to highlight and promote coexistence and peace between the people is absolutely needed."

One of the lessons about the power of good news is learned from 'Torah's Book of Numbers'. Moses sent out his twelve scouts (also known as spies) to explore the land of Canaan (the future Jewish homeland), and they brought back a report filled with both good news and bad news. On the one hand, they provided an optimistic picture of the land, extolling its agricultural potential and calling it a "land flowing with milk and honey." On the other hand, they cautioned that the inhabitants were powerful and aggressive, with fortified cities that would be daunting to conquer. In the end, the negative consequences weighed heavily on the nation. The Israelites lost faith in G-d's promise and rebelled against Moses, resulting in a brutal 40-year trek through the desert.

But amidst the gloom and the skepticism, two scouts stood out for their steadfast devotion to G-d: Caleb and Joshua. These two brave men, in the face of the other scouts' negativity, delivered a message of hope and promise. They encouraged their fellow Israelites to trust in G-d's strength and conviction, assuring them that they could take the land of Canaan with G-d's help. As a result of their unwavering faith, Caleb and Joshua were the sole survivors from their generation who ultimately entered the Promised Land, a testament to the power of persistence, devotion, and good news.

Hayvi and YALLA (Watch Yalla) can change the way people view the world around them, creating a ripple effect that can lead to greater social and political change. As a society, we should strive to seek out and share positive news, for it has the power to bring us together, spark innovation, and make the world a better place.

The Colorful Feminist

I hugged her so tight when she surprised me in Paris at my fashion show debut. She took the train from London for a short visit and then went directly back home in time to entertain guests for Shabbos.

Sharon Schurder is a high-powered banking executive by trade but a rebel artist in truth. She is a ceiling crasher and a stereotype buster, which makes her a part of my tribe. Sharon has found empowerment and a platform for self-expression through art. Her use of bright colors, intricate patterns, and expressive forms is a reflection of her love of Judaism. Her art celebrates her individuality and rebellious spirit.

She's thought-provoking yet conservative. She's spiritual yet sensational. She's both a rulebreaker and a rulemaker. She's brilliant yet childlike. She's just everything, and that everything is right on her canvases for all to appreciate.

She completely shocked me with the most honest and vulnerable answers to the questions I WhatsApp'ed her earlier this year.

Tobi, "Do you think your talent is G-d given?"

Sharon, "I really believe that everyone is born with talents as part of the plan G-d has for each one of us on planet Earth. I think the key is what you do with those talents and how they are nurtured. G-d obviously gave me this wonderful ability to express myself through art, but I didn't see it as a talent. I let it go. It was actually my mom who cheered me on, and I needed her to force me to realize my talent and what I am capable of. I explore this concept of the unveiling of talent' into the world in my latest release of paintings titled the 'Burst Collection, where I paint about the constricting feelings of fear, hurt, pain, and suffering. And hiding. Exploding into a glorious array of colors to represent the release of joy, hope, and blessing Because embracing your talent often takes bravery."

Tobi, "Do you find G-d in your color selection because you are an outrageous explosion of colors!? If so, what colors and why?"

Sharon, "10000000% G-d chooses my colors because Tobi! You have to watch me when I paint; I have absolutely no idea what I'm doing! No plan, no carefully curated photo that I'm copying, no diagram on my phone, nothing. It's just me, my hands, and G-d and together we are creating beauty. I get totally lost in the act of painting, to the point that my hands become possessed. I lose control, and the paint takes over. The actual color isn't important; it's the explosion of the various clashing and complementary colors coming together that is. It's a fabulous question, Tobi, because really you are asking, does the actual color palette of a painting matter? I always wonder about this myself. I must challenge myself in the future to paint a collection in black and white only, and then I may be able to answer more fully."

Tobi, "If you could paint a prayer for the world today, what might that look like?"

Sharon, "Peace. Peace. Peace. Peace within and peace externally. Tranquility within each and every person, love, and respect throughout the world. How have anxiety and depression become so prevalent? Why is hatred so rampant? I've actually just created a large-scale painting as part of The Burst Collection called Peace. The painting is made of resin, mica powder, paint, and shards of glass. Because that shard of glass can glisten and shine, or it can stab and harm."

Tobi, "Where do you find your inspiration for your art? biblical, spiritual, or maternal?"

Sharon, "After studying in Art School but feeling a misalignment with my values, I put down my paintbrushes in 2007. It wasn't until the tragic stillbirth of my eldest daughter in 2015 that I found solace in art again and began creating these bold, luxurious pieces using resin, palette knives, paints, and inks. It's a delight to now create on my own terms and infuse my work with meaning and light. Pregnancy loss and my desire to be a mother have definitely been shaped by work. Death changes you forever, and that chasm I still feel provides a space to explore. But I can't ignore my wanderlust too! The world is so beautiful! Lastly, I'm a massive feminist, and being an Orthodox Jewish Feminist is often a rocky journey, so when I'm faced with situations that I would love to stand up and scream about, these days, I find it safer to channel my frustrations and desire to make the world a better place on the easel."

> "The only way for a woman, as for a man, to find herself, to know herself as a person, is by creative work of her own; there is no other way."
>
> —Betty Friedan

Ty Hunter

It's not every day that you can consider Beyoncé's and Billy Porter's stylist a friend who shares faith values and a love of fashion. I didn't have to do much explaining about my mission of fusing faith and fashion because TY has been living that way all his life.

He's one of the most important tastemakers in the entertainment industry, and his work has performed on world tours, album covers, and walked the Met Gala (several times). His designs and innovative ideas can be seen in everyday life as well as in many different areas of fashion. Despite all of that, his book, 'Makeover from Within', is where he really unveils his best looks as he allows the reader to get to know the real Ty. His heart and soul are far better dressed than any celebrity on the red carpet.

I was truly honored to get him to answer my questions, as his busy schedule of book tours and upcoming talk shows keeps him jumping with close to 500,000 followers as well. I knew that no one had ever asked him questions like these before.

Tobi, "How has G-d influenced your fashion career, and how did you fuse those two together?"

Ty, "G-d has always been in my life in all aspects. The main ingredient in moving forward in anything is just having faith."

Tobi, "Do you believe your creative talents are G-d given?"

Ty, "ABSOLUTELY! I'm blessed that he places me in different situations that allow me to use all of the talent that He has given me."

Tobi, "Did you lean in on faith when styling Destiny Child and Beyoncé? If so, please provide examples."

Ty, "Of course. Knowing the show must go on and leaning on faith to see through situations. In the entertainment world, mishaps occur, but through faith, the show must go on, and things always work out in the end, a lot of the time for the better."

Tobi, "If you had to style out a world prayer, what would that look like?"

Ty, "No matter what it would look like, it would be beautiful. It would definitely be bright and peaceful. I would connect everyone with a single thread to connect all of G-d's children."

Tobi, "How do you define the term "modest attire?"

Ty, "It just depends on modest means to an individual, but for me, I believe in dressing how you feel and whatever makes you feel good. I believe in not dimming your brightness and your true self. It's ok not to blend in with the crowd, and it's ok to shine bright."

Embracing a makeover within yourself is one of the most powerful and transformative experiences a person can undergo. It requires a willingness to confront your innermost thoughts and feelings and to seek out the courage to change what no longer serves you. It means taking an honest look at yourself without judgment and being willing to see your flaws and shortcomings as well as your strengths and your resilience. With effort and dedication, Ty Hunter created an internal transformation, releasing old patterns and limiting beliefs. Embracing a makeover within yourself means taking responsibility for your growth and personal development in the most fashionable way. He realized that the power for change lies within himself, which led to a more fulfilling and authentic life.

> "The authentic path may take longer, but the moves and impact will forever be legendary."
>
> —Ty Hunter

Model Judge

In the summer of 2009, I first spotted Nolé in the background mingling with all the other guests that attended my inaugural "The House of Faith and Fashion" poolside runway show. I had hosted 200 guests to view a perfect visual representation of my newly inspired mission of combining faith and fashion. I was distracted by the judge from 'America's Next Top Model, as I was fearful that Nolé Marin would comment on the show as blatantly as he did on seasons 2, 3, and 4. Fortunately, two years later, I sat down with him on camera for an interview on my first attempt at a reality show called 'The House of Faith and Fashion'. He was the first person outside of the Jewish community and entrenched in the fashion that understood my unique, somewhat controversial, out-of-the ordinary idea. He was always thoughtful, respectful, and sensitive to the uncommon duality of my passion project. He allowed me to challenge him about beauty standards because he owned an important modeling agency. Through our conversations, I learned about his impeccable standards, which gave me insight into how he worked with his clients in the fashion and entertainment industries. Our friendship has grown over the years as I have requested his advice on fashion event productions, i.e., the controversial Park Avenue South show that challenged the New York City mayor. He was always supportive in every creative arena I asked him to step into, and he continues to be a knowledgeable source that I include in all of my projects.

I felt a sense of déjà vu as I asked him the following questions: Once again, Nolé and I are going to be on TV together as hosts of the up-and-coming TV Talk show 'The Fashion Four', along with Martu Freeman Parker.

Tobi, "Do you feel that your creative nature is a G-d given gift?"

Nolé, "I feel talent is a natural given blessing, a gift from our creator."

Tobi, "When I first reached out to you about The House of Faith and Fashion, what were your immeasurable thoughts? (2010)"

Nolé, "My immediate thoughts are: how do people combine faith with fashion? Do we combine them?"

Tobi, "What is your take on modesty? Do you feel that we all need to practice more modesty?"

Nolé, "Modesty—I personally feel it's a wonderful style. It really is the proper way to dress and create incredible stylish looks without compromising yourself."

Tobi, "How much faith do you need in yourself and G-d to make it in modeling and/or acting?"

Nolé, "Within Modeling and acting, you need incredible faith within yourself and so much more. If you don't have faith with strong beliefs, you won't reach your goal at the end of a long, hard road. Faith is the fuel to keep going."

Tobi, "Did you feel a little like G-d when you were a judge on America's Next Top Model?"

Nolé, "When I was a judge, I felt like a teacher or principal. Directing them, informing them, and guiding them along the lines of what's expected of them with the intention to nurture their best. I don't know if that's G-d like, but it's a job of authority.

Tobi, "If you could design a prayer, what might that look like?"

Nolé, "If I were to design a prayer, I would have you look into a mirror because it all starts with you! The first thought would become your prayer of the day.

Nolé Marin is a superstar style and image maker who has mastered the art of creating a distinctive and influential public persona. He knows how to use clothing, hair, makeup, and other visual elements to showcase his clients' unique strengths and personality traits while also helping to establish and reinforce their public image. Nolé knows how to build a lasting and impactful legacy for a celebrity or public figure.

What comes as a delightful surprise is that his judgement also includes inner beauty. Inner beauty refers to a person's character, personality, and values that make them a beautiful human being. It is a reflection of their kindness, compassion, and generosity towards others.

Nolé is his own best client.

Fashion Ambassador

Upon hearing my request, Edward Mermelstein, Commissioner of Foreign Affairs for New York City's Mayor Eric Adams, simply stated that there is only one person who can help me with fashion at The United Nations. I was convinced that every embassy has its own department, but I soon learned that title belongs to only one person, and that's Evie. After our initial chat, she invited me to her first ladies' luncheon during UN Week in NYC. This is the designated week that all dignitaries descend upon the Big Apple with sessions, conferences, addresses, lunches, parties, dinners, and terrific traffic jams. After I attended the afternoon gala at 530 Park Avenue, I knew why she earned that position. There is no one like Evie Evangelou, President and Founder of Fashion 4 Development.

"Fashion 4 Development (F4D) is a private sector global platform founded by EE in support of the United Nations Millennium Development Goals and "Every Woman, Every Child". The UN initiative was spearheaded by Secretary-General Ban Ki-moon. F4D builds upon the core leadership principles of the 4Es: Educate, Empower, Enhance, and Enrich, and activates partnerships that promote the fashion and textile industries. They advance economic and social development activities, preserve culture, and empower women. In 2015, F4D committed to supporting the 17 countries."

Her website is so impressive, but it can't be matched with the reality of what her global mission is.

"F4D's mission is to promote positive social change and harness the power of the fashion and beauty industries by implementing creative strategies for sustainable economic growth and the independence of communities worldwide through the expression of fashion." That's a whole lot for one sentence, and she embodies it all.

I cherish conversations that I have with industry people such as her.

Tobi, "Do you believe that G-d gave you a gift of creativity to develop your business model for fashion development around the world?"

Evie, "Absolutely! I definitely believe the passion and vision all along came from G-d alone. I asked the Divine, then waited for Him and my faith to guide me to a most successful plan.

Tobi, "How much faith do you lean on before every event you manifest, plan, and complete?"

Evie, "A great deal. If I didn't have it, I could not have made it through all the trails, tribulations, and adversity. With my faith in full force, I watched G-d open and close doors and windows in the direction that had the best results."

Tobi, "If you had to write a prayer for the world (with your business message), what might that look like?"

Evie, "Empathy and clarity—with these two traits, the world has a chance to go on. If you can empathize with your fellow human being with clarity, as you would a member of your family, then we can have a better world."

Tobi, "How did you handle the large hurdles with your health in order to push on? How did faith play a role?"

Evie, "I didn't know what was wrong with me, but I placed my undying trust in the scared heart of my Greek Orthodox religious teachings. I never lost faith through my diagnosis, treatments, and, thankfully, my recovery!"

Tobi, "How do you see faith and fashion as a combined power with your work at the UN?"

Evie, "Faith comes along in fashion in the area of making clothes, as it empowers the women around the world that craft the clothing. Fashion allows them to have faith in themselves and their abilities."

Tobi, "Can you tell me about one highlight event that G-d definitely stepped in as a co-chair?"

Evie, "My inaugural first ladies' luncheon in 2011 as my faith was there to help me pull it all off. I had no funding and no production team, yet fashion designers such as Oscar De la Renta and The UN were willing to take such a big risk with me. I worked tirelessly for 20 hours a day with my belief in G-d and my vision to accomplish a huge and prestigious event. I haven't stopped since then!"

There is an important lesson in The Torah about the term United Nations, the nations of the world.

During the holiday of Sukkot, the Feast of The Tabernacles, Jews sing Psalm 117, yearning for the day when all of the nations praise Hashem. (G-d) This particular psalm is part of the "Hallel" prayer service. While Sukkot commemorates the miraculous protection G-d provided the Children of Israel in the wilderness, it is truly meant to be a festival for the entire world. This is reflected by the 70 bulls sacrifices in the Holy Temple which corresponds to the 70 nations that make up all of mankind.

I sing praise of Evie as a person, a businesswoman, a survivor, a faith sister, and a dreamer because I know the world, and certainly the UN, would be a better place with more women like her.

The Converted

Writing about her in my first book proved insufficient for either one of us, as she continues to be a work in progress. Kate McGuire went from Mary Poppins of sustainability to Carrie Bradshaw of refashion. I know our real friendship started with two Burberry coats and an Instagram live. While I was recuperating from serious surgery, my daughter and Kate repurposed two of my favorite outerwear pieces into a one-of-a-kind masterpiece. The first time I wore it was during an Instagram live about my book, especially the essay and photo of Kate and her magical Converted Closet. Since then, she's shown her stunning stuff at 'Haute and Holy', the modest runway show on which I collaborated with Mana Fashion Services.

Kate is now the brilliant and innovative re designer that Vogue is intrigued by as she's turning season two of 'And Just Like That' into 'Who Wore Converted Closet'. "My mission is to influence," the designer states in Vogue. "I need to show people that there are alternatives [to shopping brand new]—celebrities are the people who can amplify the message more than anyone else."

We could talk for hours about G-d's place in our lives, as both of us share a deep attachment to his divine orchestration of our friendship. I might have asked her these same questions before, but each time Kate's answers develop more depth.

Tobi, "How has faith helped you through these exciting and challenging times?"

Kate, "Faith is the engine powering the McGuire machine! I'm a spiritual being with a human experience, and the resources I need to surmount any and every challenge I believe are fully alive and well within me! Life's become a journey of uncovering and remembering who I really am, recognizing the innate power I have as G-d's Flow. When I'm in a state of true surrender, challenges just don't appear! And I now recognize that when uncomfortable emotions arise, it's because I'm identifying with a limiting belief I've picked up along the way; the emotional discomfort indicates that my perspective at that moment is not aligned with G-d's; I'm trying to manipulate something to go a certain way because there's a subconscious belief that if I don't, things will go 'wrong'. Thankfully, the stronger my faith gets, the better I am at trusting in the unknown. My biggest dream is to live in a state of total surrender because I know how blissful this would actually be!"

Tobi, "Do you believe that G-d had a hand in your enormous rise with dressing Carrie?"

Kate, "G-d is The Hand! I believe everything I am, do, and have is G-d given. My work in life is to allow the flow—to stay open-minded and live in a state of positive expectation. The dream state! It's the nicest feeling anyway, so why not? The situation with dressing Carrie evolved so organically that it did feel heaven-sent. It was so obvious from the moment Danny Santiago first came around and set eyes on my converted closet that I inadvertently had Carrie's grown-up wardrobe right there! Danny and Molly Rogers are the costume creatives for the cast of 'And Just Like That', having met and worked together behind the scenes of 'Sex and The City'. The next time he came, Danny brought Molly, who got super excited, saying, "You two were separated at birth!"

and they started pulling pieces for SJ to try there and then. I even popped down to the closet in my bedroom to bring up a couple of other pieces I thought she might like! Carrie Bradshaw's fashion choices are ultimately always SJP's choices. She and I are a similar size, but most of the pieces she wore were tweaked to fit; she likes an open neckline (which I've realized is really flattering!) and has a minuscule waist. When I step back and think about SJP, the incredible global fashion icon that she is, wearing the clothes I created by converted old fashion to show what's possible and how we don't need to buy new, one can't help but wonder whether there's a bigger purpose at play here. It's my life's mission to enlighten, uplift, encourage, and entertain around this subject, and I feel I've been catapulted into a whole new level of influence as a result of this collaboration."

Tobi, "What does your everyday spiritual practice look like? Does it prepare and armor you for the real world?"

Kate, "An interesting question: what is the "real world" exactly? I'm not sure I even believe in objective reality! My spiritual practice revolves around regular, quiet communion and connection. It's about switching off the five senses and tuning into a higher dimension—a field of pure potential where G-d exists. Closing my eyes and sitting very still tells my body that we're going to a higher mind and to let go. It's important to me that I sit on a cushion and have a ritual of sorts, so my body gets the message quickly. It's amazing how much the body rules the mind! I thought it was the other way around, but I now believe our bodies are so conditioned to seek the familiar that they'll make it tricky for the mind to do anything that involves letting go! The 'unknown' is where the magic happens for me, and getting comfortable with the unfamiliar is I believe, critical to accessing and flowing with new possibilities. My imagination is so important to me, and I treat it like a muscle that needs exercising and expanding regularly. I want the imagination of a child again! I listen to a lot of recordings from spiritual teachers—30 minutes at the beginning and end of each day—to align myself. I need constant reminding that I'm surrounded by pure, unseen love, and it's always deliciously soothing."

Tobi, "Are you more convinced than ever that your talents are G-d given?"

Kate, "Everything about me is G-d given and it's such a relief to know that! I am NOT running the show! It has become clear that being able to see multiple possible different configurations of a garment beyond how it initially presents is a gift. I honestly thought everyone also did this until it became apparent through Instagram that not everyone does! And what an almighty blessing that this gift is not only extraordinarily fun and deeply satisfying but also one of the major solutions to the fashion industry's broken Take-Make-Waste model. By seeing old clothes as fabric with which to create new pieces, we'd be able to create all the new fashion the global population could ever need for many future generations and cause NO environmental damage in the making of them. When upcycling becomes mainstream, the fashion industry will transform, and a new type of creativity will rise. I'm excited about all aspects of it! Working with parameters and limitations, e.g., having finite amounts of a particular fabric, involves problem solving, and in finding solutions, new designs emerge. That has GOT to be G-d given - sustainability gifting us new heights of creativity! Yet again, G-d's gifting us beyond our wildest dreams—when we look back, don't we always see the pattern of joined dots?"

Kate needs no conversion because she is a major part of rewriting the gospel of fashion.

Aunty Sandy

She wasn't the friendliest person in the family; as a matter of fact, she could be quite scary at times. She wasn't the warm and fuzzy aunt that family gatherings usually had, especially in the Chassidish world of Borough Park, Brooklyn. She was a rebel like me, and I guess that's why we always got along. My Aunt Sandy was sassy, smart, sensible, simple, sophisticated, and saucy.

Sandy married my uncle, Chiam Roth, when I think I was about 10 years old. The only thing I remember about their wedding is that the entire family abandoned me and my other Aunt Rita for a road trip from New York to Chicago for the ceremony, as she was a midwestern bride. When I first met her, she looked like a Barbie doll, with black hair, long legs, red lipstick, and very pale skin. At that age, I related to everyone in reference to my favorite doll, which ironically, my Uncle Chiam's first wife introduced me to when I was 2 years old and obviously took hold of me ever since then.

My aunt and uncle were my exotic relatives, as they traveled to Greece regularly and shopped at Beau Brummell and Barney's. Their first apartment in Kew Garden Hills was decorated in a modern decor of black lacquer and gold, complete with an Egyptian cat statue. It was my chicest escape from my own crazy home, and I spent a lot of time there absorbing the atmosphere of floor-length fox fur coats, high-heeled cowboy boots, lush cashmere sweaters, and bell-bottom jeans.

After she gave birth to their son, Mechel (named after my grandfather), the family's life took a 360-degree turn into the

Bobov Sect of Chassidim and their move to Borough Park. Gone went the hippie chic couple to be replaced with black suits, over-the-knee skirts, and a formal dining room set and a proper china cabinet. However, no matter what modesty practices my aunt was wearing, she still swam in a different direction. Meaning, she was determined to be a powerful woman in a patriarchal shtetel of the strictest kind, and she had my full attention and unwavering respect.

She earned her first degree in nursing at the University of Illinois. I'm uncertain as to when she received her master's in hospital administration because she was a constant student, never quite satisfied with resting on her laurels. Her attitude, along with her multiple degrees, gave her entry into high-paying power positions within the nursing home and rehabilitation facility syndicate that was owned and run exclusively by men. Sandy turned the place upside down and right side up.

When her interests or hobby turned to antiquities, she preferred to get another master's degree in that area rather than relying on appraisers to inform her how priceless an artifact was. That was impressive enough, but when she got bored, is when she first started to get interesting. On a whim and a thought, she decided that instead of hiring a lawyer, she might as well get a law degree and enrolled in Fordham Law School as a night student because she couldn't interfere with her day job. Of course, she graduated with praise and moved on to a highly coveted position in a hospital. Sandy was a full-fledged superhero whose power was education. This was so contrary to her immediate environment among the ultra-orthodox that it bordered on being purely hilarious. I was watching and laughing along with her, applauding her sheer chutzpah.

She commented on every boyfriend and husband that I had because she unselfishly earned the right to do so. Sandy Roth shielded me with everything she could when my own mother abandoned me right at the age of serious courtships and upcoming marriage proposals. She knew that some sort of mother image had to step in to navigate what was occurring in my social life and into my first engagement, wedding, and marriage. My aunt would never allow Shabbos or Yom Tov to pass without including me and my devastated father in her plans. Her undertaking was enormous, as she had a big career, a husband, and a child of her own. This unselfish behavior included pleading with my father to walk me down the aisle to spare me the humiliation of my absentee mother.

No, it wasn't always a perfect relationship. We had our fights and timeouts, which included disapproving choices of my ex-spouses, my career moves, and allegiance to her husband's brother, my dad. For years, she couldn't express how she really felt about my relationship with my dad as she watched it erode into a Cinderella story of stepmothers and stepsisters without the fancy balls and handsome princes.

She morphed into a recluse as she got older, preferring her books and Hollywood gossip magazines instead of family parties and gatherings. Age was not kind to her body, yet her mind continued to be sharp.

The most meaningful exchange I ever had with her was after she read my first book, 'The House of Faith and Fashion, that was dedicated to her late husband, my Uncle Chiam Roth (ZL). She reprimanded me about this whole literary venture of mine. She cleared her throat before crying and said to me, "I always thought you were smart and creative, Tobi, but I never knew you were a genius to have written such a masterpiece. I heard your voice in every word, and I remember all the stories just as you have written them. Thank you, thank you."

That was probably the last coherent conversation I ever would have with her, as she passed away 2 years later after the COVID madness, lockdowns, and nursing home regulations. Yet, if that's the last of her sentimental lesson plans, I feel I have successfully completed my formal higher education in the best way possible. I have earned a master's degree from the University of My Aunt Sandy Roth.

Esther

To be teaching Esther Muller anything at all is quite an accomplishment because she knows everything. Her late mother's colorful description of her was how I was first introduced to her. I met her glamorous mother at a Passover Seder table in Netanya, Israel. She was clutching a small purse by Louis Vuitton and reprimanded me about my dating status. This included her chulent recipe and a speech about her daughter Esther.

After a short while, I met Esther in person and connected the dots that her mother had drawn with some added extras. I could fast forward to our private weekly Parsha (Torah portion) classes or reminisce about my 'Ethics of The Fathers' lessons to her and other female CEOs that she arranged at my apartment. Yet, I wish to start at the very bottom to emphasize her enormous heart and giving nature. In 2009, as my world seemed to disintegrate, I couldn't even remember how to use my BlackBerry or computer. My mind completely shut off as I tried to process everything that was happening to me in public and private. Seeing me in a manner that disturbed Esther so much, she summoned her assistants to go to my house daily to reteach me how to function electronically. I felt so helpless but so grateful to her in a way that I didn't share with her until years later.

We have dined and danced together with her dear husband, Ben. My husband and I have listened to her dad's (ZL) cantorial talents. As colleagues, we collaborated on NYFW events with NYC officials and teamsters' unions. Our discussions about my lesson plans for teaching a personal branding class at her Real

Estate Academy allowed me access to the most brilliant minds in New York's real estate realm.

Morphing into Esther's Torah teacher and coach was a role I never expected I'd have, but one she takes very seriously. No matter where she is in the world—East Hampton, Jerusalem, or Australia—she does not miss our weekly chat. Each session is a divine combination of Jewish teachings and current events. We solve problems with our matriarchs and patriarchs and tap into Moses's leadership abilities.

It's a big part of my weekly routine that I cherish because I learn more about Esther the mother, Esther the wife, Esther the teacher, Esther the real estate mogul, and Esther the philanthropist.

This conversation is a glimpse of what I already know so well.

Tobi, "Do you think your talents as a creative in real estate come from G-d?"

Esther, "My creativity is inspired by G-d through my parents. Especially my mom, a Holocaust survivor who was imprisoned in Bergen-Belsen and Auschwitz. Mom was an empowered woman who was given by G-d the gift of becoming a successful fashion designer with smart entrepreneurial business talent. She was my role model all my life."

Tobi, "Is your mission to sell Israel's property a holy venture?"

Esther, "My parents were pioneers in Israel. My dad fought in the War of Independence and in subsequent wars until he was wounded during the Sinai War. He then decided to leave Israel. I was uprooted at the age of 11 to live in Brooklyn. My parents ultimately became successful and returned to Israel 20 years later. I could not return with them because I married an American and I was raising my son. I believe that G-d is gifting me the opportunity through my profession to create a legacy for our children and come back home."

Tobi, "How personal are the lessons in Pirkai Avot?"

Esther, "The best lesson that my coach, Rabbi Tobi, has taught me from Rabbi Hillel is "If not now, then when," in addition to "Speak little and do much." Israel is my passion."

Tobi, "What's your main focus right now and for the next 5 years, and why?"

Esther, "My focus is to give every Jewish person in the diaspora an opportunity to create a legacy by purchasing a home in Israel and securing their future. As an educator, I always teach the story of the Holocaust and "Never Forget" From the Prophet Ezekiel: "For I will take you from the nations. Gather you from all the lands and bring you to Israel."

Tobi, "How does it feel to be Barbie's mom, especially with the characters renewed visibility?"

Esther, "As Barbie's mom, I'm proud of her mission to empower them with self-confidence and inspire them to DREAM BIG. That all girls of different physiques, races, and personalities have unique individual gifts that G-d has given them. And to create their mission for a purposeful and meaningful life."

This past spring, she sponsored a Dudu Fisher concert at The Holocaust Museum to celebrate Israel's 75th anniversary. As she stood at the podium, starting her speech, I thought I saw her mom (ZL) cheering from the front row, chanting, "That's my daughter Esther!"

Roza

In a delightful fusion of worlds, imagine a fashion business matchmaker with the wit and charm of the renowned Netflix hit "Jewish Matchmaking." Just as the hit show connects individuals seeking love, this fashion business matchmaker brings together designers, brands, and retailers searching for the perfect creative partnership. With an unmatched eye for style and a keen understanding of market trends, the matchmaker pairs complementary fashion entities, igniting sparks of collaboration that lead to stunning collections and captivating designs. This is Roza.

Roza exudes charisma and intuition, effortlessly spotting potential matches that result in unforgettable fashion unions. Much like how the Netflix series unveils heartwarming stories of love connections, Roza, the fashion business matchmaker, reveals tales of creative synergy, where designers find their perfect match in a brand that shares their vision. In the exciting realm of fashion, Roza's expertise and passion create a tapestry of innovation and success, proving that the art of matchmaking extends far beyond matters of the heart and into the world of haute couture.

Roza and I share similar views about the different realms of fashion and their deeper meanings. This led to me asking her my favorite questions.

Tobi, "How do you see the fusion of faith and fashion as you are a proprietor of all different fashion brands?"

Roza, "I often work with modest brands, so the connection is very obvious. As for the other brands and work in general, I think faith and Judaism are such a big part of my being that it affects all my work decisions. I also get very good advice from my husband, who has a very strong sense for faith and fashion! My faith helps me work with the right people; it's of course easier to work with like-minded individuals who have the same values."

Tobi, "Do you need a hefty dose of faith to make it in the fashion world?"

Roza, "Absolutely, especially these days! Faith is the best campus (moral and ethical)."

Tobi, "Why have you gravitated toward nurturing smaller brands and designers as opposed to working with one giant brand? Do you feel a sense of G-dliness doing this?"

Roza, "I believe that my talent is seeing people's potential and nourishing it. I have a motivational personality, and I am able to turn talent into a business. I started working with smaller brands because of my personal connection and emotional investment in the designers and brands. When I see financial potential in a designer, I do everything I can to help them build a long-lasting, good business. It's the most satisfying feeling to find a small brand either in Israel, Ukraine, or even Turkey and then see them in major stores across the US."

Tobi, "If you could design a prayer for the world today, what might that look like?"

Roza, "As Jews: A Prayer for Patience and Shield/Protection and

For the rest of the world, a prayer for more love with less hate."

If you have a great brand, Roza Sinaysky is your matchmaker. She will plan the dates, book the wedding hall, and send you on your honeymoon. The only thing she can't do is promise you happily ever after.

Green Dress

If a dress could launch a career, then mine would be an emerald-green embroidered silk one from Israeli designer Shoshi Yegudayov. I was asked to promote the St. Thomas University Faith and Fashion Forum (November 2022) on a local Miami talk show called The Connect Show (CW Ch 39). I knew that the dress that would impress was Shoshi's 1950s-style pinch-waist dress with exaggerated sleeves that matched my green jeweled Manolo mules. The outfit was a huge success, as I noticed the hosts concentrated more on what I wore than what I said during my segment. A few weeks later, the founder, Natalie Cargile, called me to discuss the concept of having my own TV show all about fashion.

Since then, 'The Fashion Four' has been formed, developed, and will begin shooting in the late fall of 2023.

Shoshi's green G-ddess dress has also taken me to premieres and galas. Not to mention that all my friends have become Shoshi groupies.

Shoshi is that rare balance between a designer and merchandiser. She creates with her customer's lifestyle choices in mind. Her brand has managed to lead a real revolution in the modest fashion consciousness in Israel and around the world. That's quite an unusual creative orchestration from the ultra-orthodox enclave of Bnei Brak, Israel.

Getting to ask her questions gave me extra insight into her ability to walk that line between faith and fashion.

Tobi, "Do you believe that your talent is G-d given?"

Shoshi, "I believe that my talent for creating beautiful and unique clothing designs is a gift from G-d. The ability to envision and bring to life new designs requires a level of creativity and artistic skill that goes beyond what can be taught or learned through experience alone. It is something that feels innate and comes naturally to me, and I believe that this is because it is a talent that has been given to me by a higher power. I am grateful for this gift and feel that it is my responsibility to use it to create clothing that not only looks beautiful but also empowers and inspires those who wear it."

Tobi, "What are your thoughts on modesty being dull and muted, considering your dresses sparkle and shine?"

Shoshi, "I strongly believe that modesty is not dull or dumb but rather a valuable and empowering expression of personal style and identity. While it's true that some people may view modest clothing as boring or plain, my goal as a designer is to bring innovation and creativity to modest fashion while still maintaining the boundaries of modesty.

My shiny and bright dresses are a testament to this belief. They show that modest clothing can be just as fashionable and eye-catching as any other style of clothing without sacrificing the principles of modesty. I want to inspire people to embrace modesty and to see it as a beautiful and empowering way of expressing themselves through their clothing choices. So, while some may view modesty as being dull or unexciting, I believe that it is a vibrant and dynamic aspect of fashion that has the power to inspire and transform the way we think about clothing and personal style."

Tobi, "Why did you choose the modest market?"

Shoshi, "My decision to focus on the modest market was initially driven by my personal background and cultural influences. Coming from a region where modest clothing was prevalent, it felt natural for me to pursue this style of fashion and create designs that reflected my own personal style and values. However, as I began to explore this market further, I quickly realized that there was a serious shortage of high-quality, well-designed modest clothing options available to consumers. There was a clear gap in the market that I knew I could fill by bringing my own unique perspective and creativity to the table. Moreover, I also noticed a growing demand for modest clothing among people from different backgrounds and cultures who were looking for stylish and fashionable options that were in line with their personal beliefs and values. This made me even more motivated to create innovative and beautiful designs that could appeal to a wide range of customers while still maintaining the principles of modesty. In summary, my decision to focus on the modest market was a combination of personal and market-driven factors, and I am excited to continue creating designs that celebrate and elevate the beauty of modest fashion."

Tobi, "Do you need a lot of faith to be in the fashion industry?"

Shoshi, "I believe that faith is an essential quality for success in any industry, including fashion. In any business venture, there are always ups and downs and no guarantees of success over the long term. In the fashion industry, this is even more pronounced because fashion is inherently tied to specific times and trends. If you fail to keep up with the latest trends and meet the demands of the market, you risk missing your opportunity to make an impact. That being said, I believe that faith is necessary to navigate these challenges and stay focused on your goals. It takes faith to continue pursuing your dreams, even in the face of setbacks or obstacles. It takes faith to trust in your vision and creativity and believe that you can create something that will resonate with consumers and stand the test of time. At the same time, I believe that faith alone is not enough to succeed in the fashion industry. It takes a combination of talent, hard work, and persistence to create designs that are both beautiful and commercially successful. But with faith as a guiding force, fashion designers can stay grounded in their values and beliefs and stay motivated even during difficult times."

Tobi, "If you could design a prayer, what might that look like?"

Shoshi, "If I were to attempt to design a prayer in the form of clothing, I would focus on creating a garment that evokes a sense of peace, comfort, and spiritual connection. I might use soft, flowing fabrics and earthy, natural colors to create a sense of groundedness and serenity. I would also incorporate elements of nature, such as leaves or flowers, to symbolize the beauty and interconnectedness of all things. Ultimately, however, I believe that prayer is something that transcends the physical realm and cannot be fully expressed through clothing or any other form of material design. Prayer is a deeply personal and spiritual practice that is unique to each individual, and it is something that must be experienced and felt rather than designed or created."

Tobi, "How has modest fashion changed in the course of your career?"

Shoshi, "As a fashion designer who has been working in the modest fashion industry for many years, I have seen significant changes in the industry over the course of my career. When I first started, there were very few options available for modest clothing, and what was available often lacked style and sophistication. However, over the years, the modest fashion industry has evolved and grown in exciting new directions. One of the biggest changes that I have seen is the increasing recognition and acceptance of modest fashion in the mainstream fashion industry. In the past, modest fashion was often relegated to niche markets and specialty stores, but now it is becoming more widely recognized as a legitimate and important aspect of the fashion industry. Another major change that I have seen is the emergence of new and innovative designers who are pushing the boundaries of what is possible within the realm of modest fashion. These designers are creating stunning and original designs that incorporate new fabrics, colors, and styles while still maintaining the principles of modesty.

Additionally, I have seen an increasing demand from consumers for sustainable and ethical fashion, and this trend is also beginning to shape the way that modest fashion is produced and marketed. Many designers are now prioritizing sustainable and ethical production methods, such as using organic or recycled fabrics and reducing waste and emissions. Overall, I believe that the modest fashion industry has undergone significant changes over the course of my career, and I am excited to see what new innovations and trends will emerge."

I'm looking forward to seeing what G-d has in store for me in another Shoshi Yegudayov dress.

Tracy's Production

Tracy is a fashion connoisseur and counselor who was born in Copenhagen. Inspired by her mother's background as a high-end editorial model in the 1960s, Tracy developed a love for fashion at an early age, and she grew into a respected fashion voice internationally.

She is Executive Producer and Creative Director for Fashion Week Studio in Milan and Paris. She also founded her own fashion company in Copenhagen for Fashion Week "Runway Nation". I might have sensed her pastoral background hidden underneath designer outfits and model casting, as she has the unusual gift of being divinely calm. This character fits perfectly with her other professions in counseling and spirituality. She couldn't be a more perfect guest to book a room in The House of Faith and Fashion!

She's on a structured schedule of fashion weeks in Paris, Milan, and New York, with multiple shows twice a year. No matter when I contact her, she is always so bright and cheery, contrary to the chaos around her. Perhaps I should have just permitted her to write this entire essay herself because she could write a thesis on faith and fashion. I just settled for a few of my signature questions.

Tobi, "Do you think your talents in fashion are G-d given?"

Tracy, "In a way, yes, meaning I believe anyone can, with dedication, work, practice, and mentoring, reach an ideal state where they are able to execute and fulfill their goals and maintain a high level of aesthetics in everything they do. But it takes will, dedication, and action above all else, and that I do believe is a higher power that we need to tap into within ourselves, as it lives in all of us as spiritual beings."

Tobi, "Can you tell me when you think that G-d intervened with a show that started out chaotic and turned out great?"

Tracy, "I believe tapping into our true potential as spiritual beings causes us to be able to be cause over any situation we encounter. Many times, during the production and creation of our Runway shows, do we run into situations where we feel it's going to take a bit more power right now to get through successfully, and then in deciding to make it all go right, we naturally summon our true potential, and not once has this not worked out for our team."

Tobi, "If you could compose a prayer by producing a runway show, how might that look?

Tracy, "It would definitely entail that we are all here on this earth to spread joy and aesthetics and make the world a beautiful place. Reminding ourselves of the higher purpose to create prosperity not only for us but everyone we work with and in turn inspire everyone that watches the shows to create beauty in their lives."

Tobi, "Faith and fashion are not usually teamed up; do you think that they should be?

Tracy, "I believe strongly that faith and fashion are teamed up, and so beautifully so. Faith is the true knowingness of a higher power and potential within oneself. With this activated, anyone in the fashion business, or really any business, can authentically express themselves in the most magical way. Faith takes you far and beyond, creating a world where people spread joy and beauty, and isn't that what we all want? To create a world with more beauty and more love."

I think I'm going to appoint Tracy Murray to a permanent pastoral position in the chapel on the compound of The House of Faith and Fashion.

The Plumber's Daughter

In the vast tapestry of human craftsmanship, the construction of the Tabernacle in the Holy Temple and the art of master plumbing may appear to be worlds apart. However, these two distinct disciplines share a profound dedication to precision, craftsmanship, and artistry. My late father, Abe Roth (ZL), was a master plumber who left an indelible mark in his field. As we explore the parallels between Abe Roth and Betzalel, the chief architect of the sacred Tabernacle, Mishkan, we unveil the intertwining threads of devotion, creativity, and excellence.

Exodus: VaYahel: 30-32: "G-d selected Betzalel, son of Chur to be the foreman and master of all types of craftsmanship, to devise plans, work in gold, silver and copper and do carpentry and other skilled labor." The sacred tasks of building the Tabernacle involved pipes, fittings, and copper water basins in order to construct G-d's traveling abode while roaming through the desert and during the construction of the first and second Holy Temples.

Abe Roth's journey as a master plumber was paved with a profound understanding of his craft. His meticulous attention to detail, whether working on complex plumbing systems or the most straightforward installations, was nothing short of awe-inspiring. His technical expertise ensured that every project he undertook was executed flawlessly, leaving a lasting impression on those he served. I am told stories about his mastery till today. Much like Betzalel's unwavering commitment to constructing the Tabernacle (in Hebrew, the Mishkan) with divine precision, my dad's work was infused with a similar sense of devotion.

He approached each project with a dedication and respect that transformed plumbing from a mere trade into an art form. My dad's devotion to his craft was evident in the sanctity he brought to every project.

The art of master plumbing and the design of the Tabernacle and Mishkan both demanded a fusion of technical expertise and artistic flair. My dad was not merely a plumber; he was an artist in his field. His ability to find innovative solutions and seamlessly integrate plumbing with architectural designs showcased his creative vision. Every project became a canvas for Abe's artistry, and the end results were transformative.

My Dad was the first orthodox Jew to receive his master plumber's license in the 1960s. He was a trailblazer in so many ways by learning his craft as a pipe fitter in the US Navy on board the fighter ship SS Kittywake. I recall my father telling me of the hardship of surviving on only eggs and dairy products during his military service as kosher food was not available and he was a Torah-observant Jew coming out of the yeshivah world.

Abe Roth (ZL), founder of A Roth Plumbing and Heating, was a formidable force standing at 6 feet 2 inches, balancing a cigar in one hand and a wrench in the other, with a voice that could fill a room.

Growing up under the watchful eye of a master crafter and leader certainly nurtured my creative side, and for that I will remain eternally grateful.

My guess is that, with G-d's grace, when Moshiach arrives to build the third and final Holy Temple, He will call upon my dad for some good plumbing advice.

My Prayer Warriors

During my stay at Mount Sinai Hospital, recovering from a major operation and hooked up to medical machinery, I meticulously planned my Seudah Todah, a lavish banquet of gratitude. Knowing that planning this party was crucial to overcoming my current struggles, I followed the sage advice of my dear friend and Breslov lecturer, Gedale Fenster, by preparing for my future cheesecake party.

While slowly pacing the sterile hospital corridor, willing my muscles to cooperate, I carefully crafted the menu, decor, and guest list for my upcoming event. Settling on a date for the party was not easy, but I eventually chose a day that gave me ample time to recover from the grueling side effects of chemotherapy, allowing me to regain my health and strength.

Hosting my Seudah Todah felt like having all the rarest and most precious gems in the world gathered together in one place as my guests. The diverse group of 35 remarkable people came together that evening, and their joy and happiness for my well-being were palpable. As we dined and danced beneath the starry sky, I took a moment to acknowledge the invaluable contributions of each guest to my journey. These incredible people had become my armor, my dream coat, and my cozy blanket in the face of illness and recovery.

For those who have read my first book, they will recognize these exceptional individuals as my Prayer Warriors. I had carefully selected the best of humanity, inviting them to join my WhatsApp group, where together we shared sincere prayers, uplifting Torah lessons, and delicious challah bakes. The group also fortified me with Tehillim (Psalms), top-rated doctors, and adjunct therapies. Indeed, this group was more than just a collection of individuals— it became my support network and a shining example of what humans can accomplish when they come together.

Astar Nussbaum, Family Member, Special Education Teacher

Betty Makovsky, Family Member

Catherine Underwood, Brand Licensing Executive, Retired VP of Licensing Union Bay

Ceilee Sitt, Event Planner and Philanthropist

Chanie Einhorn, Real Estate Management

Debra Rabinowitz, Family Member

Donna Schneier, Family member and Founder of Donna Schneier Fine Arts and Bijoux Contemporary

Dr. Rabbanit Adena Berkowitz, Psychotherapist, Lawyer and Founder of Kol HaNeshmah, Senior Educator at the Manhattan Jewish Experience

Dr. Rachael Shindler, Nutritionist

Elizabeth Sutton, Artist, Entrepreneur and Founder of Elizabeth Sutton Collection

Esther Muller, Senior Global Adviser to Sotheby's International, President of the Academy of Continuing Education, Real Estate

Georgie London, Retired Executive in Communications

Hillary Barr, CEO of R New York Real Estate Brokerage

John Henry Edington III, Makeup Artist and Stylist

Mimixa Patel, Executive Assistant to The House of Fashion and Fashion book projects

Natalie Packer, Owner, Packer Ford and Lincoln Auto

Rebbitzen Miriam Yerushlami, Author, Lecturer and Therapist

Rebbetzin Sara Shulovitz Vorhand, Criminal Attorney, Rebbetzin of the Congregation Heichal Moshe

Sarah Rabbani, Event Planner

Shevy Shanik, Founder of Shevy Shanik Events

Alvina Alston ; CEO More Media

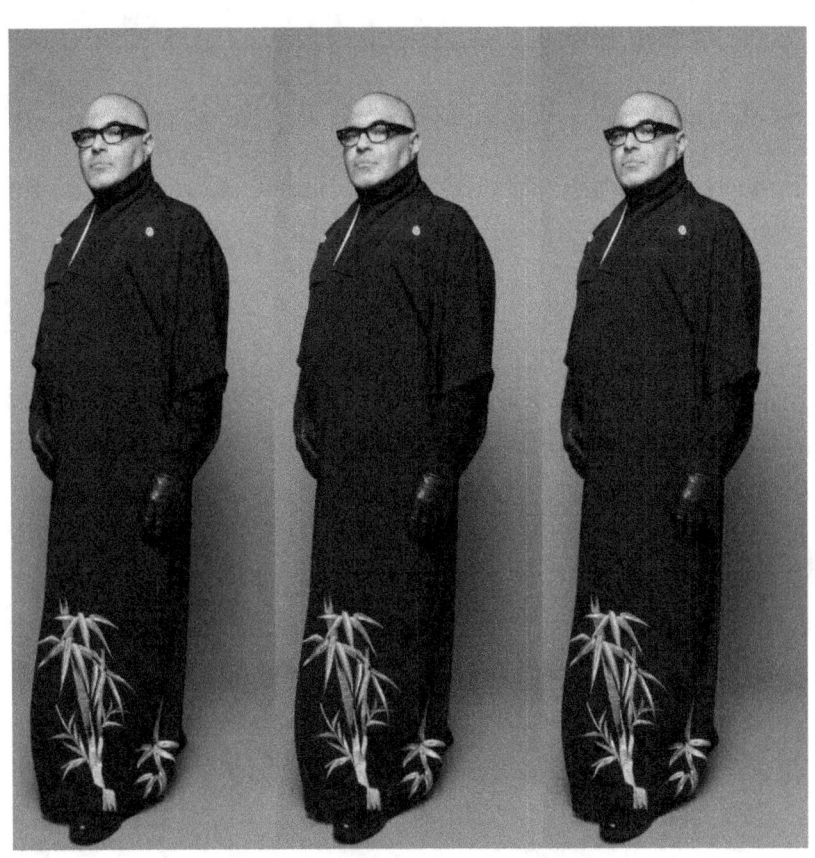

Photos courtesy of Nolé Marin

Talya Bendel

Talya Bendel

Photo courtesy of Fashion 4 Development

Photo courtesy of Fashion 4 Development

Photo courtesy of Ty Hunter

Photo courtesy of Sharon Schurder

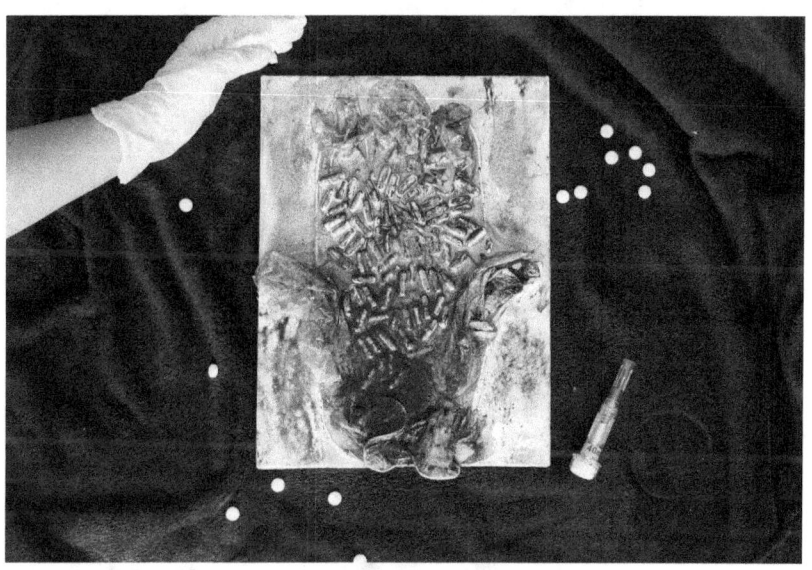

Photo courtesy of Sharon Schurder

Tobi Rubinstein and Abe Roth 1990

Aunt Sandy Roth and Tobi Rubinstein 1984

Esther Muller

Kate McGuire from Converted Closet

Photo courtesy of @hayvi_bouzo

Photo courtesy of @tracy_murray

Roza Sinaysky

CHAPTER 5

STARTING A NEW CHAPTER

"Faith allows you to say goodbye to the past, and at the same time open new doors to the future."

Gedale Fenster

Photographer: Iris Hyde

This was the speech I gave at my 65th birthday party, hosted by Elizabeth Sutton and Esther Muller. The celebration included 50 of the most diverse friends that I am blessed to have.

"Thank you all for being here with me, but the truth is I'm here because of all of you. My favorite book is 'The Ethics of the Fathers,' a powerful collection of tractates written in the second century. In it, it proclaimed that if there are more than three people in a room, G-d's wisdom must be shared. In the fourth chapter, it is known in the very first sentence that Ben Zoma teaches four great lessons that are summed up in four big questions. Who is wise? Who is strong? Who is rich, and who is honored?

These are his answers: Who is wise? He who learns from every person. Who is strong? He who subdues his evil inclination. Who is rich? He who is happy with his lot. Who is honored? He who honors others.

Let's unpack this tonight because that advice spans from one end of this beautiful home to the other.

According to me, who is wise? Well, I think that at 65, I may finally become a wise woman. If indeed I did, it was because I learned from all of you: Rabbis, Rebbetzins, lawyers, teachers, real estate moguls, stylists, doctors, superstars, wives, mothers, and dear friends.

Who is strong? We all fight battles every day with the other side. Sometimes they win, but hopefully most of the time they lose. Pardon me for inserting my own version of strong, but surviving stage four cancer is strong, thank G-d. Marrying and divorcing till I got it right is strong. Starting the 'House of Faith and Fashion' when no one understood me is strong. Breaking every stereotype and glass ceiling for an Orthodox Jewish woman, is strong. Not being concerned about what everyone thought and knowing that only G-d has my full attention, is strong.

Who is rich? Boy, did I learn lessons on that one. I finally consider myself a billionairess, as I look across the room and see the riches of my friendships.

Who is honored? I've been in the company of many honorable people in my lifetime. But tonight, I'm honored to be the fairy g-dmother of our hostess, Elizabeth Sutton. I'm honored to be a teacher, friend, and mentor to Esther Muller. I'm honored to be the mother of my wonderful child, Lola. I am honored to be the wife of my handsome Latin hubby, Felipe. Most certainly I'm honored to know each and every one of you and share in your accomplishments, your failures, your passions, and your poisons, your hopes and your dreams. I bless all of you for allowing me to be part of your lives.

Happy birthday to me!

ACKNOWLEDGEMENTS

"Thankfulness has an inner connection with humility. It recognizes that what we are, and what we have, is due to others and above all, to G-d."

Rabbi Lord Jonathan Sacks (ZL).

Chief Rabbi Pinchas Goldschmidt, President of the Conference of European Rabbis

Rabbi Shalom Arush, Author, Founder of Chut Shel Chessed Institutions

Eli Goldsmith, CEO of Unity Souls Projects

Rebbetzin Rochie Pinson, Author

Regina Rubinov and Dimensions Therapy by Yuval Levi

Yitzy and Rosie Weinberg

Rabbi Leibel and Shaina Stolik, Chabad of South Palm Beach

Uriel Setareh

The Mauthner Girls, Susan Toline, Debbie Klein, Linda Weiler

Rabbi Benjamin and Avital Goldschmidt, Altenu Synagogue New York

Gedale Fenster, Motivational speaker, Founder and CEO of the People's Insurance Claim Center and Evolutions Treatment Center

Jean Alerte and Jickael Bazin, Citadelle Publishing, Founder and ACA Branding Agency

Dr. Carol Aghajanian and team at MSK

Orner Families, Eli Orner and family, Shimmy, Debra Orner and family, Dr. Gabi and Mindy Orner and family

Aid L' Shalom; Devorie Neuman Hartstein and Gitti Klein

RCCS Rofeh Cholem

Shainy Batshevah

Mana Fashion Services

Dr. David Shafer

Elissa Ciment

Liana Zavo, Zavo PR

Rabbi Yoshiyahu Yosef Pinto

Sharona Abraham, Owner of Sharona's Dough to Go

Derrick Hammond, CEO of 20/20 Vizion Entertainment

THEHOUSEOFFAITHANDFASHION.COM

The goal of this book is to reveal G-d's presence in fashion, jewelry, art, beauty and style through the lens of Jewish teachings therefore elevating each creative process to divine proportions.

Instagram @tobi_rubinstein

Don't forget to start from the beginning. Order book one today!

www.ingramcontent.com/pod-product-compliance
Lightning Source LLC
Chambersburg PA
CBHW060917120626
46553CB00001B/355